# STRENGTH

# STRENGTH

*Encouragement, and Comfort through Transition, Trial and Trouble*

## DR. CASEY R. KIMBROUGH
### CHARLOTTE, NORTH CAROLINA
### 2013

Unless otherwise indicated, all Scripture quotations are taken from the New Revised Standard Version of the Bible.

# STRENGTH
## ENCOURAGEMENT, AND COMFORT THROUGH TRANSITION, TRAIL AND TROUBLE

For more information featuring the author,
Contact Reverend Dr. Casey R. Kimbrough on the World Wide Web at www.Aliveteachingministries.com or by mail at Alive Teaching Ministries, 14115 Northridge Dr. Charlotte, North Carolina 28269

caseykimbrough@gmail.com
DrK@aliveteachingministries.com

Or

www.Mountcarmelbaptistchurch-nc.org
PastorK@mountcarmelbaptistchurch-nc.org


ISBN: 978-1-937183-63-9

Printed in the United States of America

*Dedication to three generations of women*

*who lived faith before my eyes....*

*Cora Lee Weatherly (My Great Grandmother)*

*Delores BedDard (My Grandmother)*

*Delberta J Kimbrough (My Mother)*

*Thank you for the years of love and support.*

# ACKNOWLEDGEMENTS

My life and journey of faith has been enriched by countless numbers of people who have poured into my life. The names are too many to list, family, church community, educators, who have help to shape me into the person that I am today. I am obligated to give thanks.

I give thanks to God who created me in the mind of God and gave expression through the creative act of life. I am grateful to my parents Mr. Archie and Delberta Kimbrough who valued their boys Casey and Archie above all. I am thankful for my brother Archie J. Kimbrough who has protected, provided, and poured immeasurably into my life. I am grateful to my second set of parents Rev. James and Eunice Walker; their love and support can never be repaid. I am grateful to my great grandmother, Cora Lee Weatherly who has been the greatest spiritual influence on my life.

I am grateful for the love of my life, LeeDonna W. Kimbrough who has been my best friend, partner, and an extraordinary mother and wife. I thank God daily for our children Casey Jr., Alexander, and Rebecca who have taught me how to love unconditionally.

I thank God for all of my mentors and teacher who have poured spiritual wisdom into my life. Thank you, Dr. H. Beecher Hicks Jr, Senior Minister of The Metropolitan Baptist Church, Washington D.C. for taking a chance on a young seminarian and allowing me the privilege to learn in a ministry of excellence. To my colleagues and comrades of the faith, I thank you for your love, support, and pursuit of The Kingdom of God.

To my church family, The Mount Carmel Baptist Church where God has privileged me to serve as pastor for now over 22 years, I thank you for your prayers, support, and love. You have been my crucible, school house, and spiritual family allowing me to mature in the Word and Spirit of God.

*Thank you for loving God, loving others, and following Jesus.*

Development Team

A special word of appreciation is extended to the following persons for all their help and encouragement.

Mr. Kenston Griffin - My Personal Coach
Dream Builders Communications

Dr. Jeffery Leak - Edit Advisor
University of North Carolina at Charlotte

Ms. Tonya Allen - Edit Advisor
Dream Builders Communications

Mr. Lex Kimbrough - Cover Art/Design
Voice, Rhythm Vision

Ms. Vera Jackson - Technical Support
Mount Carmel Baptist Church

Mrs. LeeDonna W. Kimbrough
Alive Teaching Ministry

# The 23rd Psalm

## *A psalm of David:*

*The Lord is my shepherd; I shall not want.*
*He maketh me to lie down in green pastures,*
*He leadth me beside the still waters.*
*He restorth my soul.*
*He leadth me in right paths for his name's sake.*
*Yea, though I walk through the valley of the*
*shadow of death,*
*I fear no evil;*
*For thou are with me;*
*Thy rod and your staff, they comfort me.*
*Thou preparest a table before me in the*
*presence of mine enemies;*
*Thou anointest my head with oil,*
*My cup runneth over.*
*Surely goodness and mercy shall follow me;*
*All the days of my life;*
*And I shall dwell in the House of the Lord*
*forever.*

(The King James Version is simply beautiful, and
cannot be duplicated for its pros. This is the Version
I learned as a child.)

# The 23rd Psalm

*A psalm of David:*

*The Lord is my shepherd; I shall not want.*
*He makes me to lie down in green pastures,*
*He leads me beside the still waters.*
*He restores my soul.*
*He leads me in right paths for his name's sake.*
*Even though I walk through the darkest valley,*
*I fear no evil*
*For you are with me;*
*Your rod and your staff, they comfort me.*
*You prepared a table before me in the presence*
*of my enemies;*
*You anoint my head with oil,*
*My cup overflows.*
*Surely goodness and mercy shall follow me*
*All the days of my life,*
*And I shall dwell in the House of the Lord my*
*whole life long.*

(This is the version of the academic community, The Revised Standard Version.)

# *Contents*

# *The Lord is My Shepherd*

DR. CASEY R. KIMBROUGH

# INTRODUCTION

One of my earliest memories as a child is sitting on a church pew listening to the sound of thunder, or what I thought was thunder but in actuality was the sound of the preacher's voice. Like so many who have gone before me, I was marked by the voice of the Church and thus set loose on my odyssey in search of God.

I am a child of the turbulent sixties, in the year that Dr. Martin Luther King Jr. was assassinated April 4, 1968, I was seven years old and can vividly remember watching on television an interview where Dr. King sat in his study lined with books as he talked about the civil rights movement, his vision and the beloved community.  Dr. King was in my young estimation the most impressive, intelligent, articulate man I had ever seen.  Yes, I was impressionable.  I can remember thinking, "one day I am going to have a room full of books."

It was from an improvised community in Pittsburgh Pennsylvania, in what is known as the hill district that I made this observation. Not many days thereafter walking to school one morning I noticed men in army fatigues, with fixed baronets standing on the street corners of our neighbor.

What I would come to learn later, is that those solders were young men from the National Guard sent to be certain that black people from the hill district did not come downtown inflaming violence that had engulfed our nation.

Nineteen sixty eight was the year riots swept across America in the inner cities; the black community, our nation was being torn apart, and my young heart was broken. I could not figure out for the life of me why anyone would want to kill such a wonderful man, the Reverend Dr. Martin Luther King Jr.

It was in this same season of life, the person who was the most important spiritual influence of my young journey, my great grandmother Cora Lee Weatherly passed. She was a humble southern woman who migrated from Roanoke Virginia and carved out life with her husband, who had already passed by the time I came to know her. In the often harsh environment of the steel city, Pittsburgh Pennsylvania Cora would sow in me the seed of faith. To this day, I am utilizing the lessons of faith this wise yet, unassuming Christian women planted in my life.

In the context of the Church, communities such as Sixth Mount Zion Baptist Church, Macedonia Baptist Church, and New Bethel Baptist Church I listened to the preaching/pastor and Sunday school teacher who help me to understand: "God so loved the world that he gave his only Son, so that everyone who believes in him may not perish but have eternal life." (John 3:16) We were taught in difficult and dangerous times God was with us and no matter how dark the night, hope in Jesus, declared that with each dawning of a new day, the love of God could heal every broken heart. Yes, my young wounded heart would experience the gift of healing, and my mind was regularly challenged, inspired by the mystery of God. I am a child of God, the unique blend of Christian faith, temper in the heated crucible of transition, trail and trouble within the heart of the African American community.

Engaged in pastoral ministry for over 22 years, I have witness Gods vision that all would have the opportunity to mature in faith through the study of the Word of God, celebrate God in Worship, and serve God through ministry. To this end, I am convinced that Martin Luther, the protestant reformer, got it right, when he called people of faith "the priesthood of all believers." We are the children of God; we affirm that all believers have the privilege of a relationship with God, and the Word of God. In the context of the preaching/teaching ministry I have sought from week to week to help create an environment where those who seek God could encounter the Word of God, and the opportunity of a divine experience.

## Strength

Simplicity is a lost art. We the Church have too often been guilty of complicating faith. Too often we have majored in the minors and minored in the majors. I recall learning that the bible was written at a six-grade level. When I first heard this I was shocked, especially given that I was in seminary and investing three years of my life seeking to understand and communicate to others the boundless treasures of the Word of God.

"Strength" is my attempt to share some of the lessons that God and life have taught me in the context of the faith community. I have sought to share the words of God in a simple manner applicable to life. My goal is to get out of the way and allow God to be heard and experienced.

The pastor's study is the place where I retreat seeking God first, before ever engaging the text or the community. Preaching is an art, an imperfect art in which the sermon is always in process. Immediately, after walking out of the pulpit, having shared what in my estimation is my best effort, my mind races over the possibilities of how I could have elaborated on this point or that point more clearly. Ask any preacher, they will share with you, that they are never quite satisfied with the sermon that was offered up. Each week the preacher struggles, how can you tell the greatest story ever told, when it has already been told by the greatest teacher ever, Jesus? The preacher learns to trust the grace and spirit of God, in Gods strength the preachers weakness is made prefect.

God has ordained through the simple humble act of preaching that men and women would be offered the mystical opportunity of salvation. I count it a great privilege to have had the opportunity to share the Word of God in the pastoral context for almost 25 years.

While all sermons are particular in the context in which they are presented, sermons at their best ought to speak to the universal concerns of the human family. The birth of children, food, shelter, protection, community, loss of life, as well as seeking to understand the meaning of life; the joys and sorrows of the human experience are universal thus the presentation of the Word of God has the potential to speak to every fiber of the human family.

Preaching at its best involves painting on the canvas of the heart and mind. Preaching is God's mystical opportunity to share with others the presence and story of an invisible God. When there is no hint of Gods spirit, words become heavy and cumbersome, when Gods spirit breaks through the words become light flowing like streams of living water. Preaching at its best is born out of the experience of sorrow, joy, heartbreak, healing, lose and love. In the living of life, we are led to prayer, many have learned to call on God through tear stained eyes. God does some of God's best work in seasons of transition, trail and trouble.

Foundational to our seeking God is spiritual relationship. Intimacy is the accent of spiritual relationship, a way of knowing, being still, listening, speaking, and moving in conversation with God. Our goal is not to learn religion, ours is to maintain our relationship, to ever commit to the conversation. The knowing experience, this intimacy with God begins with awareness, a hungering, and thrusting of mind, body and soul.

## The Book of Psalms

The Book of Psalms is full of all human drama. We read the psalms with our head and heart. I confess that the psalms are one of my favorite books of the bible. The psalms express a community's joy and sorrows, the psalms were Israel's prayer and praise book. The book psalm, this ancient book was shared within the context of the urban community of my youth with passion, hope and love.

As a child it was the stories of David, David the shepherd who fends off wild animals, David standing in the face of Goliath victoriously, David and Bathsheba, David the shepherd boy who would be King. It was through these stories that my youthful faith was born and nurtured.

Now, having lived a half century plus, the God of David is still my hero, ever with me on my journey of faith and life. The promise of God through the voice of the 23rd psalm is: when confronted with tough times, seasons of transition, trail and trouble we are not alone. God is with us.

The 23rd psalm is a timeless document, a spiritual poem of epic proportion, a classic of inspiration that is without equal. Here is a psalm of confidence; rich in metaphor, giving witness to a life lived in loving, trusting, and faithful relationship with God.

It has been said that the best interpreter of scripture is scripture. I encourage each of us to read and reread the 23rd psalm and allow the majesty, mystery and the spirit of God to minister to your soul.

While most of this material has been birthed out of the sermonic presentation, I have made adjustments for the media of print. I am keenly aware that preaching is an imperfect art, and yet it is through the foolishness of preaching that God chose to offer the gift of salvation. I offer this in all humility, not as an academic exercise, but as an offering of love.


In this book you will be encouraged, comforted, strengthen and challenged to claim your strength.

I pray that your determination is heightened to maintain your conversation with God.

Yes, you are stronger than you realize.

Claim your Strength!

Claim your Strength!

*God!*

# CHAPTER I

## The Lord is My Shepherd

My first introduction to the 23rd psalm occurred at a young age in a Sunday school class room. I cannot remember how old I was, but I do remember that everything in the room was big. The room sat in the lower level of the church. People buzzed around like something important was about to take place. There was a kind of organized chaos. In this environment it felt like no one was in charge but, everyone seemed to be in charge. The teachers were people who my grandmother had regular conversation with and I was keenly aware that I had better be on my best behavior.

We entered the room, a damp smell was in the air, and the walls were dual, painted but needing to be repaired. Pictures of places and people lined the walls; I did not recognize the people or the places; pictures of far way places, fields, shepherds, water, blue skies, images of Jesus, David, and others from the ancient world. The bee hive of activity was interrupted; then, I heard the words, "the Lord is my shepherd I shall not want."

The 23$^{rd}$ psalm opened to me a new world. A world where I was introduced to David the shepherd boy, a young lad, with many older brothers; David was a care giver, and had a heart like God's own heart. David a shepherd boy, young, innocent, thrust into conflict with a bully, a giant named Goliath, David, the boy who would one day become King of Israel was the hero of my childhood.

Year after year, I would hear and learn more about David the author (historical) of the 23rd psalm. Years later I would discover that the 23rd psalms had captured my imagination, stolen my heart, and introduced me to the God of the bible. Like so many others who had gone before me I was marked by the stories of the bible and thus set loose on my odyssey in search of God.

What an odyssey it has become, I have sought to live a life of faith, a faith that has been grounded in the stories of the bible as I have journeyed on my quest to know God. It was my introduction to the stories of Abraham, Isaac, Jacob, Noah, Moses, David and Jesus that fueled my belief and trust in the God of the bible.

My faith as a child may have been simple, never the less it was faith. In the simplicity of childlike faith I received the story of the 23rd psalm as the foundation upon which I would start my quest to know God. There is not a day that goes by when I do not thank God for those who introduced me to the 23rd psalm. The 23rd psalm has been an invaluable part of my life. When I eulogized my grandmother, father and mother, I did not rely primarily on my seminary training or theological education; I reached back to the stories of my childhood and called up what has been the most important encouraging and comforting words in my life. On more occasions than I can number I have found strength in the words of the 23rd psalm.

> *"The Lord is my shepherd; I shall not want.*
> *He maketh me to lie down in green pastures,*
> *He leadth me beside the still waters.*
> *He restorth my soul."*

Who among us when we have lost love ones to that great enemy called death; grandparents, parents, spouses, children and love ones - have not turned with tear stained eyes to these timeless, powerful words: *"The Lord is my shepherd?"*

Twenty five years I have been eulogizing the beloved of God. I cannot count how many times I have brought families, broken hearts, wounded of soul and tear-stained eyes, in to the presence of God with these simple but spiritually powerful words.

> *"The Lord is my shepherd."*

Pulling out of rich depths of the story of David, and the 23$^{rd}$ psalm, genteelly guiding the grieving by hand to the presence of God, it has been my privileged to be present with those who have suffered loss, heart break and disappointment. Serving as pastor (shepherd) is a unique gift only a few of the elect will know this privilege. People are generally kind to you, they invite you into the very special times of their lives, the birth of children, the blessing of babies, graduations, weddings, family celebrations, as well as the great challenges of their lives; broken relationships, job separation, and the loss of love ones.

David was a shepherded, Jesus said, "I am the good shepherd," both witness to the strength of God in the context of the struggles of life. David's witness moves our hearts and spirit in ways that outpace our human reasoning and understanding. David speaks to our soul. Our soul is refreshed. "As a deer longs for flowing streams, so my soul longs for you, O God." (Psalm 42:1) Let, the healing begin claim your strength in God.

## The Shepherd

David with a soul that hungers after God affirms that you can depend on God. David reminds us that the shepherd positions, the shepherd provides, the shepherd protects, *"the shepherd leads to green pastures, and the shepherd leads beside still waters."* The shepherd God leads to green pastures the place of peace, rest, and security.

The shepherd God leads to waters of quietness, refreshing streams, and gentle breezes. All symbols of the sweet spirit of God. The shepherd God surrounds us, wind, and water, are symbols of the presence of God.

*"The Lord is my shepherd I shall not want."*

I shall not lack any good thing. All that God desires in my life shall come to pass. It is the shepherd God who watches over me. All that God desires shall come to pass. What God has for me, is for me. In my times of anxiousness, when the chaos of life is swirling about, in danger, in distress, here is when the shepherd God takes me by the hand and leads me.

*"The Lord is my shepherd, I shall not want he makes me to lie down in green pastures. He leads me beside still waters, he restores my soul he leads me in the path of righteousness for his namesake."*

*"He restores my soul."*

The shepherd God refreshes, revives, invigorates, rejuvenates, restores, revitalizes.

Life takes, God restores.

Life keeps taking, God keeps restoring.

Life wounds, God heals.

Life keeps wounding, God keeps healing.

17

Life desires to hold me captive, God desires my deliverance.

The Lord is my shepherd; I am wholly, completely, utterly, absolutely, fully, dependent upon the Lord.

Remember the words of Jesus, "I can do nothing on my own." (John 5:30a)

*"The Lord is my light and my salvation whom shall I fear? The Lord is the strength if my life; of whom shall I be afraid"* (Psalm 27:1-2)
*"The Lord is my shepherd."*

*Yea though (*I like the King James Version here) *I walk through the valley of the shadow of death, I will fear no evil' for thou art with me; thy rod and thy staff they comfort me.*

The shadow of death means that death may be close. Death casts its shadow but death cannot touch me. Death is near but I shall not fear! Why? God's got me. God's got me. The shadow of death in the text can be translated dens darkness. Like a heavy fog that is upon us as a weight.

Not long ago in my office I sat listening to a young woman who was going through a very painful divorce. It was evident that her heart had been broken, her life was in crisis. Not only was she dealing with the loss of a spouse, but the implication of the loss emotionally, financially, and spiritually was now placing an enormous amount of pressure on her. In the mist of telling her story he said, Pastor I feel like I have a gorilla sitting on my chest.

Our first ministry to those who are hurting is to be present. Next, we must listen without judgment, in a spirit of love. As I reminded this young woman, you are a child of God. You are loved by God. Whatever you go through the promise of God is "I AM WITH YOU!"

> *"Who will be able to separate us from the Love of God? Will hardship, or distress, or persecution, or famine, or nakedness, peril, or sword? No, in all of these we are more than conquerors, through him who loved us. For I am convinced that neither death nor life, neither angels nor demons, neither present nor the future, nor any powers, neither height nor depth, nor anything else in all creation, will be able to separate us from the love of God that is in Christ Jesus our Lord." (Romans 8:38)*

Remind yourself daily when you are going through transition, trail, or trouble - no adversary, no valley, no mountain, not even death will be able to separate me from the love of God.  No I belong: you belong, we belong to the shepherd God.  God does some of Gods best work when trouble is all around.  Remember, Moses standing between the red sea and Pharaohs army pressing down upon him and the people.  God speaks; Moses what do you have in your hand.  Stretch out the rod in your hand. (Exodus 14:21-22)  Beloved, use what you have, what you need God has already place in your hand.

### Thou preparest a table before me in the presence of mine enemies;

The Shepherd God *(Yahweh)* welcomes me, welcomes you and I, a gracious host is our God. Welcome into the house of God, welcome to the temple of God, welcome to the presence of God. We are God's guest; the Lord invites. I am a guest, you are a guest, we are honored guests at the table of the Lord, it's the Lord's Table, God prepares the table, and all that is on the table has come from the Lord's hands.

It is the Lord who fills my cup! It is God's way of saying; you will see the goodness of the Lord in the land of the living. No, I do not have to die to see the goodness of God. I will see the goodness of God in the land of the living.

I remember talking with a senior citizen who was a long time believer. The conversation was such that she recited many of her struggles through life, giving witness that God has been faithful and brought her a mighty long way. She talked of how she was severally ill when she was a younger woman, and how at the time she was concerned about the welfare of her young children. She talked about how the Lord put food on her table, and shelter over her head provided a means for her to care for her young family. She reminisced over her transitions, trails and troubles how at every point God had been faithful. Then she said quite un-expectantly, "Pastor, God does not have to take you to take care of you."

***Thou preparest a table before me in the presence of mine enemies;***

Oh, yes, enemies are at the table. Oh, yes, they surround us, oh yes the adversary is planning and plotting or destruction. But, the enemy cannot harm me. The enemy cannot harm you. Look at the table; keep your eyes on the table.

Whatever you may be facing today fear, anxiety, sickness, loss of job, loss of relationship, loss of health, or the loss of a loved one – but, keep your eyes on the Lord.

Keep your eyes on the Lord.  Your enemies cannot stop God from preparing the table. Your enemies cannot stop God from inviting you to the table.  Your hope, your strength, your blessings are not in your enemies hands but in the hand of the Lord. Keep your eyes on the Lord.

> *Surely goodness and mercy shall follow me;*
> *All the days of my life;*
> *And I shall dwell in the House of the Lord forever.*

Goodness and mercy will follow me.  Goodness and mercy will track me down.  Wherever I go, wherever you go, wherever the children of God go; the shepherd is with us, "lo, I am with you always, even unto the end of the world." (Matthew 28:20)

Everything I am.

Everything I hope.

I am in the Lord's hands.

I am invited to the Lord's Table.

I eat the Lord's food.

I drink from the Lord's cup.

I dwell in the Lord's house.

Thus, with the psalmist,

**I will bless the Lord at all times.**

**His praise will continually be in my mouth**

**My soul will make her boast in the Lord**

Let the afflicted hear and rejoice

Oh, magnify the Lord with me let us exalt his name together.

O taste and see that the Lord is good.

O taste and see that the Lord is good. (Psalm 34)

## Psalms 23

*The Lord is my shepherd; I shall not want.*
*He maketh me to lie down in green pastures,*
*He leadth me beside the still waters.*
*He restorth my soul.*
*He leadth me in right paths for his name's sake.*
*Yea, though I walk through the valley of the*
*shadow of death,*
*I fear no evil;*
*For thou are with me;*
*Thy rod and your staff, they comfort me.*
*Thou preparest a table before me in the*
*presence of mine enemies;*
*Thou anointest my head with oil,*
*My cup runneth over.*
*Surely goodness and mercy shall follow me;*
*All the days of my life;*
*And I shall dwell in the House of the Lord*
*forever.*

DR. CASEY R. KIMBROUGH

# CHAPTER II

## I SHALL NOT WANT

I entered the humble home, welcomed by her gracious daughter who gently leads to her ill mother's bedside. I have the privilege to serve as her pastor, and now she is not many days hence from death. With endearing eyes she looks at me, her fragile voice breaks through the silence. "Pastor, thank you for coming, God has been good to me, I have had a good life."

She has not resigned herself to death. The cancer has been robbing her day by day of her strength. With her physical strength diminished, her faith is strong. Her life has been lived in the simplicity of faith, trusting the word of the sacred text. "The Lord is my shepherd; I shall not want."

In life's journey we all will have occasion to seek understanding in the midst of a difficult situation. At the core of faith is the reality that faith does not answer the question why, faith is a question of trust. "I will trust you Lord!"

# Listening

Faith encourages us to listen. Faith encourages us to be still, listening for what the voice of God is saying. Listening for God begins with being still. "Be still and know that I am God." (Psalm 46:10). When we are still, from the quiet place of our soul, we are prepared to ask the questions of faith.

What am I hearing?

What am I observing?

What direction is God leading?

Listening helps us discern who God is in light of authentic biblical interpretation, and positions us to respond to the guidance of God

We read in Psalm 23:1 "...*I shall not want.*" Yet, when we look at our lives we think, "But I do want." Many of our wants are connected to that which we perceived as good; health, long life, to witness our children mature, and to see the blessing of grand children. Is the psalmist suggesting that if we have faith in God faith will extinguish our wants (desires) and we will be content with what we have and long for nothing more?

There are some religious voices that teach renunciation as the key to happiness in life. Desire nothing and you will never miss anything you do not have. Love no one and no one will have the power to hurt you by not returning that love. Teach yourself not to love life too much and death will hold no terror.

Is this what the psalmist suggests? A theology of renunciation robs us of the sweetness of life. Teaching us to connect with no one and to love nothing, I am certain this in not what God has in mind. Jesus modeled and taught that we are to connect with God, and connect with others. *"By this everyone will know that you are my disciples, if you have love for one another." (John 13:35)*

Part of our challenge with this text "I shall not want" is our understanding and choice of translations. The four hundred year old King James translation of the bible uses words that mean something different in 21st century English than they did in the late 16th century. The intent of the Hebrew is more accurately captured by some recent translations:

*"...I shall lack nothing." (World English Bible)*

*"...The Lord takes care of me as his sheep; I will not be without any good thing." (Bible in Basic English)*

*"...The LORD is my shepherd; I have everything I need." (New Living Translation)*

*"...The Lord is my shepherd, I don't need a thing. (The Message)*

# I Lack Nothing

The writer of the psalms (David) refuses to split things into spiritual and material. There is no separation of need in God. Verse one "The Lord is my Shepherd" affirms that God (Yahweh) is the satisfaction of all wants and needs. God is our portion. God is all sufficient in the midst of spiritual, material, physical, emotional need. It is through relationship with God all our needs are filled.

The church of my childhood was fond of saying, "God may not come when you want him, but God is always on time." Their faith understanding was born out of the harsh realities of life. In the midst of struggling for daily necessities, food, shelter, clothing, they appropriated into their faith a God who was not only capable, but also willing to meet every kind of need. The image of table, "you prepare a table before me, in the presence of my enemies, my cup overflows." We must resist the temptation to over spiritualize images of table and cup. The psalmist has known the experience that God put real food on the table; God put real drink in the cup. God provided not only in the spiritual world but as well in the physical. Any who have ever lived from pay check to pay check, experiencing more month than money understands this with greater fervor! God provides!

## God Provides

This line (I shall not want) of the 23rd psalm is the writer reminding us that God is faithful. God provides not only in the spiritual world, God provides in the physical world; food, water and a warm safe place to rest. The phrase, *"I shall not want,"* is inspired by the experience of the Israelites wandering in the desert, when God provided for their needs 40 years; supplying them with food, water, and a daily place of rest, so they lack for nothing.

When placed in the context of Israel's community of common memories of faith. Exodus 16 reminds us of God's blessings of manna, the surprising bread of heaven, the resolution of hunger, God's children will not lack.

*"Surely the Lord your God has blessed you in all you're undertaking; he knows your going through this great wilderness." (Duet. 2:7)*

Faith is the understanding that the food I eat, the water I drink, the clothes I wear, all come from the hand of God.

*"The Lord is my shepherd, I shall not want."*

I can give witness with so many others, that God will provide. When I think back over my journey, of where God has brought me from, out of urban poverty, through inner city schools, educated without adequate resource. I graduated from some of the finest educational institution in this land. I have been privileged to serve as the Pastor of one of the finest communities of faith in Charlotte, teach in the University, and influence many lives to help usher in the Kingdom of God. I am thankful for the many opportunities I have experienced and understand them as a gift of God. It is not that I am so gifted, or so righteous; no like so many others I have had many challenges and made many mistakes. I can honestly say that God has been faithful! My life like so many others is a testimony to Gods amazing grace. Yes, I can witness that God provides. Yes, God provides.

## Unanswered Prayers

I am reminded of the story; a woman in her mid forties sees a man at a community event that looks vaguely familiar but she can not quite place him. She then realizes that as a young girl she had a crush on him in the seventh grade. Every night this thirteen year old girl would go to sleep praying that God would make him love her. Her prayers went unanswered - she never understood why God would not grant the heartfelt prayer of a devoted thirteen year old girl. Now, thirty years later and observing what this man (unanswered prayer) has grown up to become, when she looked at him, she understood that some of God's greatest gifts are unanswered prayers.

The great protestant theologian Paul Tillich, writing in reference to the messianic hopes, writes, "Although waiting is not having, it is also (a kind of) having. The fact that we wait for something shows that in some way we possess it." Waiting for God is our affirmation of trust in God.

We all have struggled with the notion of wanting more and our desires for more. If "more" means only more wealth, more fame, more power, new automobiles, bigger houses then our soul is in an unhealthy place.

But if more means seeking the Kingdom of God, more wisdom, more love, more peace, more courage, more generosity, more resources to enhance human life and help relieve human suffering, then our desires are not misplaced. Part of me never wants to be satisfied with whom I have become and what I have achieved. There is a part of me that continues to seek more of God. If in writing this book I can help someone through their time of transition, trial, or trouble then my desire to write will be worth seeking more.

Our challenge is to want more of that which will bring glory to God. The early Church fathers said it best. What is the chief end of man? "Man's chief end is to glorify God, and to enjoy him forever." To this end we live.

Glorify God!

Enjoy God!

Celebrate life!

Live!

Love!

Laugh!

Glorify God, by being the unique created one that God has designed.

You are created in the image of God.

You are stronger than you think.

Claim your strength!

Claim your strength!

# STRENGTH

# CHAPTER III

## HE RESTORES MY SOUL

My first memories of praying are that of a little boy, kneeling down at the side of my bed, with the gentle cool fall breeze blowing through the windows and the voice of my great grandmother Cora Lee Weatherly, kneeled down beside me lovingly instructing, "Baby fold your hands, and lets us say our prayers."

The first prayer that I was exposed to, I remember like it was yesterday:

*"Now I lay me down to sleep,*
*I pray the Lord my soul to keep;*
*If I should die before I wake,*
*I pray the Lord my soul to take.*

This classic prayer from the 18th century was taught to me by a senior lady who was born in the late 1800's in a small southern community in Roanoke, Virginia, she died in the early 20th century having migrated to the mountains of Pittsburgh, Pennsylvania. While she had a limited formal educational, she had a well developed spiritual awareness. I often think of her, what her life must have been like. When I met her she was then the saintly grandmother who was the

34

core of our family's spiritual reservoir. I could see from her hands that life had not always been easy for her. I later would learn that she had worked as a domestic for many years, cleaning and ironing clothes for wealthy families in Pittsburgh.

When she would lead me in prayer she would say, "Baby do not be afraid, talk to God just like you talk to other people, you can tell God anything." These earlier lessons of prayer were so lovingly engraved on my soul that now almost a half century later these lessons of prayer form the foundation of my understanding of prayer. This humble small statured elderly woman would be my greatest spiritual teacher. It was through her daily lesson of faith that I was first introduced to the soul.

What is the soul? Let me suggest that the soul is that which makes us human and separates us from all other living creatures.

> *"And the LORD God formed man of the dust of the ground, and breathed into his nostrils the breath of life; and man became a living soul."*
> *(Genesis 2:7 KJV)*

To our knowledge human beings are the only animals on the planet that practice religion. Thus, we are reasonably safe in asserting that religion is a uniquely human endeavor.

The soul represents everything that elevates human beings and what it means to be created in the image of God.

## God Creates

A careful reading of Genesis reminds us that God spoke when creating the animals by saying "Let there be..." but when God created his crowning jewel of humanity - God formed from the dust of the ground Adam (humanity), breathing "ruhah" (the breath of God) life in Adam. Thus, there is a little essence of God within all of us. I love the imagery of the great American poet James Weldon Johnson

The Creation...

Then God sat down On the side of a hill where He could think; by a deep, wide river He sat down; With His head in His hands, God thought and thought, till he thought, *"I'll make me a man!"*

Up from the bed of the river God scooped the clay; And by the bank of the river He kneeled Him down; And there the great God Almighty Who lit the sun and fixed it in the sky, Who flung the stars to the most far corner of the night, Who rounded the earth in the middle of His hand; This Great God, Like a mammy bending over her baby, Kneeled down in the

dust toiling over a lump of clay till He shaped it
in His own image;
Then into it He blew the breath of life, and man
became a living soul. Amen. Amen.

"The Creation" is reprinted from The Book of American Negro Poetry. James Weldon Johnson. New York: Harcourt, Brace and Co., 1922.

It is my great joy to be the father of our three children. My wife and I have two sons and one daughter. Each of our children represents a unique gift from God. I am aware that they are a unique mixture of their mother, father, and the divine mystery of God. We as parents are co-creators with God. The work of creation did not end when they were born, in many ways it begin the next dimension of life.

All life comes from God and we should receive life as a gift. In my priestly function I am privileged to bless and present children before the Lord. In the context of this scared ceremony I remind the parents who have come to present their gift of life before God and community. "To ever be mindful that while this child comes through you the child does not come from you." The child is ever to be treated as a gift from God. God gives the gift, it is then up to us to live as good stewards of the gift that God has provided.

Your life is a gift from God. No matter what you may be going through, remember that as long as you have breath in your lungs there is hope. You may not know how to access have the strength that you need, yet look to your source. Your source is your creator. Your source is God the creator of the universe. When you connect with God you connect with your strength.

The strength of God is within you. You have the power to create and recreate who you are; your last chapter has not been written. Today, begin the process of creating the life that you have dreamed. Plant in your mind and spirit the dream, fertilize it with prayer, love, faith, planning and they move to action. After that first action, then pause, reflect, evaluate the results that you are getting. If the results are not what you desire, (change) try again. Seek God, dream again, sow your dream in the field of your spirit and mind, and cultivate it with love, faith, joy - plan then move into action.

**Create**

Every act of creation begins in the spirit and mind. You must see it first in your minds eye, and then share that vision in such a way that others can envision with you and help move that vision into the physical world. Leaders cast the vision, communicate the vision, organize the people and the resources to the fulfillment of that vision. Leadership is all about vision. "Where there is no vision the people perish…" (KJV) The most effective leaders are those who with grace, influence, guide; clarify the vision and help lead to God's preferred future.

Yes, you can do this for your life. If you are not experiencing the life that you desire, you can change it. You have the power! Pray, seek God for a vision of your new life. Plant that vision seed in your mind and spirit. Fertilize that vision with love and great faith (persistence). Next, every morning you get up move into action.

Our church community now sits on forty plus acres; God blessed us with a multimillion dollar campus. When our church community begin to envision a new home there were many who joined with us, prayed, planned, and rolled up their sleeves, giving time, talent, and resources. It was my task to lead us through a process that would take approximately seven years for us to envision a new campus and a worship center. I would be the first to confess this was not an easy task. There were days of joy, but there were many days of frustration and heart break. I learned so much through this journey. At times I was popular in the church community and at other times I was unpopular. I witness the best in people but I also witness the worst in people. I saw people who I cared for deeply leave the church and yet I also saw God send new people with new vision. There were days when I was absolutely convinced that we were on the right path, and then there were days I had to fall on my face before God with tear stained eyes confessing, "We are not going to make it without you." Yet, through it all, God was there, and in the darkest of moments God taught me and our church community about the necessity to depend totally on God. Today, I can give witness that the word of God is true, "…I am with you always…." (Matthew 28:20)

Today we worship in our new multi-purpose family life center. God is faithful.

When you create, know that opposition is to be expected. Generally many people prefer to be lazy of mind and spirit, they choose not to be creators, they prefer to critique what other women and men of vision have released into the universe. It is always easier to respond to what someone else has initiated. Do not look outside your creative mind, your God destiny is in your spirit and mind. The Kingdom of God is within.

The first act of being co-creator with God is to respond to the voice of God and join with God to create your new life. Jesus calls us out of the darkness into the marvelous light. God will help us create a life that will give glory to the name of God. It is from this transformed place that we are released to create in the universe. You are not in competition with anyone. Only you and God can create the life that God has imagined. You are a co-creator with God.

Out of our deep understanding of God as creator, the giver of our soul, we call to God, knowing innately that the giver of our soul is able to keep our soul, and is able to restore our soul. It is later in the 23rd psalm that the writer declares, 'my cup runneth over." This is an act of worship; God the creator is the God who is the "restorer of the soul." The worshiper is responding to the miraculous experience of waking from the slumber of sleep, greeting a new morning. Every day is new in God. Our Sunday morning worship is a celebration of life. Sunday morning is a time of spiritual and psycho-physical healing.

The psalmist, having survived the long night, the night presented as a mini death, he wakes restored on the morning. One can almost hear the excitement in his voice; "I am alive; I have survived, I greet the new day." I woke up this morning, my mind ordered, my body is strong, I have the use of my faculties, it is a new day, a new opportunity awaits, today I shall live, love, laugh and thank you God.  My soul is for restored.


## The 27th Psalm

The 27th psalm speaks to faith in tough times. The psalmist expresses great confidence in the Lord, certain of Gods protection, thus compelling one to worship the Lord.

*The Lord is my light and my salvation whom      shall I fear?*

*The Lord is the stronghold of my life, of whom shall I be afraid?*

*When evil men advance against to devour my flesh, when my enemies and foes attack me, they will stumble and fall.*

*Though an army besiege me, my heart will not fear; though war break out against me, even then will I be confident.*

*One thing I ask of the Lord, this is what I seek; that I may dwell in the house of the Lord all the days of my life, to gaze upon the beauty of the Lord and seek him in his temple.*

*For in the time of trouble he will keep me safe in his dwelling; he will hide me in the shelter of his tabernacle and set me high upon a rock.*

*Then my head will be exalted above the enemies who surround me; at his tabernacle will I sacrifice with shouts of joy; I will sing and make music the LORD. (Nrsv)*


"The Lord is my light and my salvation whom shall I fear?" Recall David who stood before Goliath as a young lad. David that would fend off wild animals and one day is pursued by King Saul who sought to take David's life. David express' supreme confidence. "The Lord is my light and my salvation whom shall I fear?"

David is a man of faith, and will not be reduced by his fears. David understood that it was his connection with God that brought him supreme confidence. Fear flows out of a sense of being disconnected from God. "The Lord is my light and my salvation whom shall I fear?"

The plane took off; there was no hint of the sun. The sky was gray and overcast and the afternoon seemed as if early evening had already arrived. I looked for the sun only to see the gloom of the clouds which hung like they were heavy upon springs.

Yet, the higher we traveled the brighter the day, the clouds seemed slowly to evaporate higher and higher we climbed. One by one the clouds, dissipated, until the sun gently broke through, a dark day was now full of light. The sun was there the whole time the difficulty was I could not see the sun. When we cannot see the sun it is so easy to think that the sun is not there. We must remind ourselves when we cannot see the sun; it does not mean the sun is not there, we need to reposition ourselves to a higher elevation so that we can see the sun.

## He Restores My Soul

**"He restores my soul."** I read a story of a group of tourist on a safari in Africa. They hired several native porters to carry their supplies while they traveled. After three days, the porters told them that they would have to stop and rest, Explaining. "We have walked too far too fast and now we must wait for our souls to catch us." We must be careful not to become consumed with the cares this world; we neglect our spiritual life, our soul. Spiritual leader who serve long term learn the necessity of self care. Balance must be established, while caring for others we must also prioritize our health, mind, body, and soul. Every once in a while we must pause and let our souls catch up. What can we do?

We can develop a devotional life, a spiritual life; a life lived loving God and loving others.

1. A life of prayer.
2. A life of integrity.
3. A life of spirit.
4. A life of service.
5. A life of compassion.
6. A life of Word.
7. A life of worship.

We are told in Exodus 20, *"remember the Sabbath and keep it holy."* The Sabbath was given as a gift from God. The people to whom the Sabbath was first given grew up as slaves in Egypt. God said to them, *"Now therefore, if you obey my voice and keep my covenant, you shall be my treasured possession out of all the people."(Ex. 19:5)* in the movement from bondage to freedom God gave the gift of Sabbath, the gift of worship. The Jewish family welcomes the Sabbath as a reminder of liberation from Egyptian slavery. For the Christian, Sabbath worship is a reminder of our liberation from the physical and spiritual slavery of sin.

In the act of worship the Lord restores our soul. God is the one who replenishes the soul on the Sabbath.

God, in Exodus brings us the Sabbath:

> *"You shall keep the Sabbath, for this is a sign between me and you throughout your generations, given in order that you may know that I, the Lord, sanctify you. You shall keep the Sabbath, because it is holy for you…Six days shall work be done, but the seventh day is a Sabbath of solemn rest, holy to the Lord."* (Exodus 31:13-15 NRSV)

**Worship Restores Our Soul**

Luke tells us the story of Jesus' dining in the house of a Pharisee named Simon. A woman of questionable reputation (church tradition ascribes her as a prostitute) has somehow found her way into the house of this respectable Pharisaic leader. Arriving, at the feet of Jesus, we are told that she weeps buckets of tears. She then takes and pours expensive oil on Jesus' feet kissing them and drying his feet with her hair.  The host, who is the Pharisee named Simon, begins to protest, informing Jesus, this woman is a "sinner." Jesus replies, yes, you are right her sins are many, and her debts are great, and who then will have the greater love. The answer comes forth the one who has the greater debt forgiven.  Simon you offer no hospitality as I enter your house, you did not anoint my head with oil, and she has not stopped kissing my feet. Jesus tells her, *"your sins, which are many, have been forgiven; hence she has shown great love."*

> *God is love,*
>
> *Today,* know that God loves you.
>
> If you need strength right now, this very moment: repeat out loud until you feel your strength increase.
>
> God loves me.
>
> God loves me.
>
> God ***restores my soul."***
>
> I am a child of God.
>
> I am a child of God.
>
> God loves me.
>
> God loves me,

# STRENGTH

DR. CASEY R. KIMBROUGH

# *You Can Make It!*

# CHAPTER IV

## STRENGTH - GOD IS ABLE

*"Though I walk through the valley of the shadow of death…"*
*Even though I walk through the darkest valley, I fear no evil; for you are with me; your rod and your staff— they comfort me. (Psalm 23:4nrsv)*

*Yea, though I walk through the valley of the shadow of death, I will fear no evil: for thou art with me; thy rod and thy staff they comfort me. (Psalm 23:4kjv)*

Whenever the question is asked, "can God," the answer is always yes. Yes, God can! Can God hold back the flood, yes God can. Can God turn night into day, yes God can. Can God heal the wounded soul? "Yes God can!" This is the testimony of faith "yes God can." What is impossible with man is possible with God. "Jesus looked at them and said, for mortals it is impossible, but not for God; for God all things are possible." (Mark 10:27)

**The God Who Is Able**

The very name of God tells us, that God is able to do whatever God pleases, a name God first revealed to Abraham. God promised to make Abraham (Abram at the

51

time) the father of a great nation, and naturally Abraham needed a son in order for that promise to come true. Abraham and Sarah, with the help of Hagar, sought to bring forth God's promise, introducing Abrahams and Hangars child, Ishmael, into this world, planning he (Ishmael) would be the son of promise, but God told Abraham that Sarah would bear a son Isaac and through him the promise would be fulfilled.

Abraham was ninety-nine years old and Sarah was ninety, God intervened, God broke into their world.

*Now when Abram was ninety-nine years old, the LORD appeared to Abram and said to him, 'I am God Almighty; Walk before me, and be blameless, and I will make my covenant between me and you, and will make you exceedingly numerous. (Genesis 17:1-2)*

*God said to Abraham, "As for Sarai, your wife, you shall not call her Sarai, but Sarah shall be her name. I will bless her and moreover, I will give you a son by her, I will bless her, and she will give rise to nations; kings of people shall come from her." Then Abraham fell on his face and laughed, and said to himself, "Can a child be born to a man who is a hundred years old? Can Sarah, who is ninety years old, bear a child?" And Abraham said to God, "O that Ishmael might live in your sight!" God said, "No, but your wife Sarah shall bear you a son, and you shall name him Isaac." I will establish my covenant for his offspring after him. (Genesis 17:15-19 nrsv)*

One of the names of God is El Shaddai, which means God Almighty, the God who can do anything God wants to do, and yes God can give babies to couples in their nineties! God is almighty, all-powerful. El Shaddai - the name of God is used 47 times in the Old Testament and always in reference to God. It has a New Testament equivalent, which is used 10 times, meaning literally "to hold all things in one's power." Scripture is punctuated with references to God's omnipotence from beginning to end. God is the Lord strong and mighty (Psalm 24:8). Power belongs to God. (Psalm 62:11) "Great is our Lord, and abundant in strength." (Psalm 147:5) The psalmist wants us to know the God who is able to do anything. The Psalms writer affirms with certainty that God is able.

## The Psalms

David, the writer of psalms (historically attributed) who story is told out of the context of a loving relationship with a God who is able. We recall the confident boy, and King Saul, when there are none in the camp that will face the mighty Goliath of the Philistine army.

*(I Samuel 17:32) 32 David said to Saul, "Let no one's heart fail because of him; your servant*

*will go and fight with this Philistine." **33** Saul said to David, "You are not able to go against this Philistine to fight with him; for you are just a boy, and he has been a warrior from his youth." **34** But David said to Saul, "Your servant used to keep sheep for his father; and whenever a lion or a bear came, and took a lamb from the flock, **35** I went after it and struck it down, rescuing the lamb from its mouth; and if it turned against me, I would catch it by the jaw, strike it down, and kill it. **36** Your servant has killed both lions and bears; and this uncircumcised Philistine shall be like one of them, since he has defied the armies of the living God." **37** David said, "The Lord, who saved me from the paw of the lion and from the paw of the bear, will save me from the hand of this Philistine." So Saul said to David, "Go, and may the Lord be with you!"*

David having lived in the caves of Adullam when he would later be pursued by this same King Saul who sought to take David's life: it is out of the context of David's experiences these sacred words leap from the pages of our text.

*Yea, though I walk through the valley of the shadow of death, I will fear no evil;*

The very reading, the very speaking of these words brings a comfort and strength that cannot be articulated. There are some things that one cannot articulate, because one does not have the word skill to match the psycho-spiritual dynamic of life that has been experienced. One receives these healing words as a gift from God.

*Yea, though I walk through the valley of the shadow of death, I will fear no evil;*

The astute biblical student understands that here is the hock upon which the entire 23rd Psalm hangs. Here is the most poignant part of the Psalm. In the fourth verse our soul is riveted to the pages of the text. "Yea, though I walk through the valley of the shadow of death, I will fear no evil".

The 23rd psalm is a timeless document, spiritual poem of epic proportion, which bears witness without commentary. Here is a Psalm of confidence; rich in metaphor, bearing witness to life lived in trusting relationship with God. The Psalm asserts with surety, that you can trust God. It leaves not room for doubt or question. You and I may have doubt or question, but the psalm writer has no doubt or question. Let, me affirm with the psalmist, you can trust God, God is able!

*Yea, though I walk through the valley of the shadow of death, I will fear no evil;*

## In The Valley

The valley is not described, yet we know through biblical scholarship the reading of the Septuagint (the Greek speaking bible) the expression "shadow of death" is a single phrase not associated with death but more accurately translated, "dense darkness." Thus, the King James Version translated this, "the shadow of death." The revised standard, the more scholarly version translates this verse, "darkest valley." The heavy darkness that sits upon me that weighs me down.

The Revised Standard Version is the preferred scholarly version, the version preferred in the academic communities. The New International version the more common version uses the classical language, "shadow of death." Like many of you, my preference goes back to the classical version The King James version, because this is the version that my grandmother made me learn when she placed me on bended knee. "You will memorize the 23rd Psalm." Those old believers felt like there were certain scriptures that you were to memorize. I can still hear her voice.

"I don't know where you are going to go, or what you're going to do, but there will come a day when you will find yourself walking through the valley of death and you need to be able to call from deep within. Yea, though I walk through the valley of the shadow of death, I will fear no evil."

Here is where we cannot afford to error with contemporary Christianity. We cannot teach people that you are going to have your Bible with you at all times, you just pull your Bible out and hit the adversary with the Word. What happens when you do not have your Bible with you? We must hide the Word of God in our heart! The adversary will sneak up on you, when you least expect, and without no Bible in hand. The adversary does not care about Sunday morning religion. The adversary will challenge you all week long. Yes, there is some scripture worth memorizing, it must become a part of your very fiber and be planted in your spirit, mind and heart.

Now, I must confess, whenever I get troubled, I never recite the Revised Standard Version. I have graduated from three Universities; I have been privileged to sit with some of the best scholars in the land. But, whenever I get in trouble, when I need the Word, I hear in the voice of my youth, "Yea, though I walk through the valley of the shadow of death." It is not my academic training that I call forth, it is within the delicate psycho-spiritual world that I travel that I hear the voice of these words; "Yea, though I walk through the valley of the Shadow of death, I will fear no evil; for thou art with me; thy rod and thy staff they comfort me." (Psalm 23:4kjv)

Like many others my preference is to read it in the King James Version, it holds to the poetic flavor that speaks within the context of my experience. It helps me hold together that delicate balance between my past, present, and future. It speaks to my head and my heart. It reminds me that God is able!

**God is Able to Do**

Israel has experienced her seasons of lament. Israel has known Jewish suffering, hurt, alienation, and death. The experience is not unique to Israel; we also know the pain of suffering. Our community story is birthed out of suffering. We are the protégée of those who were snatched at night from the mother continent, chained, shackled, and stolen away into the dark abyss of the transatlantic slave market. Slavery, Jim crow, segregation, separate and unequal, southern poverty, northern ghettos, oppressed; economically, politically, physically and spiritually, we know suffering nationally as well as through our personal experience.

My celebration is born out of my experience. Up out of my experience God gives me a reason to celebrate. Out of the freedom that God has brought to my mind, my spirit, my soul, my life, here is where my celebration resonates out of.

We know... We Know... We Know...! I know! I know! We testify with great passion, we tell our story, "God is able!"

My critics, they say Reverend you are too passionate, you are too loud, you are too long, you "ain't" got to do that, give us a lecture, and send us on our way, twelve minutes would be appropriate, given the educational context we have been to Howard, and Harvard we have been to this school or that school. I can appreciate their right to critique my passionate proclamation. Yet, preaching at its core is passionate proclamation. When I think of the goodness of the Lord and all he has done for me, my soul cries hallelujah.

My passion is born out of my liberation; I understand where I come from. I understand who I belong too. I understand what I had to come through to stand in the pulpit on Sunday morning. I did not just fall from heaven to stand on this spot. I have had hills to cross over; I have had valleys; I had to come through transitions. I had trials and temptations. I have had to bear my cross. Like many here today I have been through some trouble. Yes, there is still some trouble I am going through. I have not made it yet. But, every day with God's help I am getting stronger and stronger.

Not just me, my mamma, my grandmamma, my daddy, and my granddaddy, it took us a long time to get where we are today. So, if I get too passionate, excuse me, my love for the God who liberated me, my love for those who have gone before, just will not let me hold back. I have got to "say it. I have got to "say it." If I do not praise him; did not I hear, Jesus declare the rocks will cry out!

My love will not let me act like I have been to the University and nowhere else. Before, I went to the University, I walked the mean streets. Before, I got in the class room, old women prayed over me. Before, I got in the cafeteria they gave me corn bread and beans. When I say that God is able, I do not need approval - God is able. I am talking about what I know already.

We are told in theological circles that God is omnipotent, meaning that God is all powerful. God is able to do. The New Testament word 'to be able" means "to have power" (dunamai the verb form for that familiar Greek noun, dunamis), when we read that God is able to do something it means God has the power to do it.

God is able to create - Creation Story.

God is able to Liberate (set free) – Israel exodus.

God is able to work a miracle – Moses at the red sea.

God is able to topple giants – David and Goliath.

God is able to do anything but fail.

God is able to supply our needs.

"And God is able to provide you with every blessing in abundance, so that by always having enough of everything, you may share abundantly in every good work." (2 Corinthians 9:8)

God is able to save us.

"Consequently, he is able for all times save those who approach God through him, since he always lives to make intercession for them." (Hebrews 7:25).

God is able to keep us from sin.

"Now to him who is able to keep you from falling, and to make you stand without blemish in the presence of his glory with rejoicing, to the only God our savior, through Jesus Christ our Lord, be glory, majesty, power, and authority, before all time and now and forever. Amen." (Jude 24).

God is able to deliver us from death. Daniel's three friends (Shadrach, Meshach, and Abednego) facing the heat of a fiery furnace, heated seven times hotter than normal. They boldly declared to King Nebuchadnezzar, "If our God whom we serve is able to deliver us from the furnace of blazing fire." (Daniel 3:17) God may choose, or God may not, yet God is able. God is able to deliver us if God so chooses.

Jesus affirms that God is able. The writer to the Hebrews said, "In the days of his flesh Jesus offered up prayers and supplications, with loud crying and tears, to the one able to save him from death…". (Hebrews 5:7)

## I will Fear no Evil

*Yea, though I walk through the valley of the shadow of death I will fear no evil.*

I rely on God completely. God is my champion. God is my transformer. The Psalmist does not mean there is not death in the valley, nor does he suggest that there are not enemies that lie in wait. What the writer affirms is that death and the enemies they lay wait in the valley, are powerless to hurt and to wound us. The writer is not denying the reality of evil. The writer suggests that he is "Gods protected child" Solidarity to Yahweh who is not only powerful but also strong. Thus, as we walk through every dark situation, example walking through the valley of the shadow of death; there are threats on every side, the enemy is laying wait, the enemy wants to ambush. The enemy wants to take everything from us. The enemy wants to take our mind, our body, our soul. The enemy wants to take our joy. We walk through the dark dense heavy valley in solidarity with God.

The psalmist says I will not fear. How can I walk through the valley of heavy darkness not being able to see, knowing that the enemy is in the valley, I cannot see all of the traps that the enemy has set for me? I will not fear. I cannot see. I know there are traps. Even death lingers, but I will not fear.

Yahweh has the power, thus, I cannot see, but Yahweh can see. God has night vision. The prophet of old tells us that God has night vision. "We walk by faith not by sight." (2 Corinthians 5:7)

I am strong, why, because God is strong.

I have strength, why, because God is my strength.

I am in complete solidarity with God.

God is able! I can sleep at night like a baby. Why, because God has me covered. God is with me.

It is God's companionship that transforms every situation. It does not mean there are no deathly valleys or no enemies. But, they do not have power over my life. It is in knowing, experiencing the powerful loyalty and solidarity of God (Yahweh) that brings us strength.

**Thou Art With Me**

**Yea, though I walk through the valley of the shadow of death, I will fear no evil.**

The promise of God's presence is the source of our strength. The joy of the Lord is my strength. I have been strengthened, some have sought to intimidate, and others to bully.

You better be afraid. I'll put a curse on you. I will do physical harm to you. Sometimes physically, other times in writing or in the spiritual world! The enemy seeks to intimidate, and rob us of our faith and peace. We learned to place our trust in the presence and power of God. Out trust is not placed in superstitions or luck. No, we are people of faith.

Faith in God!

God is wonderful!

God is amazing!

God has awesomeness!

God speaks and light shines

God speaks and oceans part!

God speaks and living beings come into creation!

Isaiah said it this way in Isaiah 40.

(Isaiah 40:1-2)

*"I waited patiently for the Lord;*

*He inclined to me and heard my cry,*

*He drew me up from the desolate pit,*

*Out of the miry rock,*

*Making my steps secure.*

*He put a new song in my mouth,*

*A song of praise to our God.*

*Many will see and fear,*
*And put their trust in the Lord.*

When I think of the goodness of the Lord, how do I respond?

What is my best action?

My best action is, to make my way to the house of the Lord.

Too take my place in the assembly.

Too lift up my broken hands.

Too announce to the world that the Lord is good and worthy to be praised.

It is not a physical location.

It is not based on brick and mortar.

It is not whether you are Baptist, Methodist, Presbyterian or Catholic.

The strength does not come for location; it comes for the vitality of relationship.

That's when the transformation takes place.

That's when you discover there's more to life than serving yourself.

That's when you learn, even though you walk through the valley.

When the enemy has laid traps for you, one after another.

The enemy is waiting in the darkness on either side to rob you of everything that God has given you.

The enemy wants to take your joy.

The enemy wants to take your blessing.

The enemy wants to take your light.

The enemy wants to take your testimony.

When you walk through the valley, the enemy wants to steal everything that you have.

I heard that the devil is a liar.

The devil is a trickster.

The devil has no authority.

The enemy only has permissive authority- that which God permits.

When you walk through the valley;

Knowing that the enemy is on either side;

Death will not take you until God give it permission.

Death cannot put its hand on you.

You may be sick, but it does not mean you are going to die.

You may be wounded today; it does not mean you are going to die.

You belong to God who made heaven and earth.

You are God's child.

God's got his hand on you.

God's got you covered from the top of your head to the bottom of your feet.

Next time you walk in the valley

Pick your head up.

Put your shoulders back.

He walks with me.

He talks with me.

He tells me that I am his own.

Jesus is in the valley with me.

Jesus is in the valley with me.

Jesus is my new life.

Jesus is my liberation.

Jesus is my deliverance.

Jesus is my Salvation.

Jesus is my Resurrection.

Jesus is my Light.

Jesus is my Salvation.

Jesus is my Strength!

Jesus is my Strength!

Jesus is Able!

DR. CASEY R. KIMBROUGH

# CHAPTER V

## GOD IS WITH ME

*Psalms 23:4b"I will fear no evil for you are with me."*

## God Is With Me

Recently, I was teaching a class in a University setting. It was a small class that focused on the spiritual life of the students. In the class, one of the students came to class late, bowed her head and sat pensive in the back of the room and not interacting in the class. This student normally was communicative, responsive, and engaged in the class dialogue. Today, she was the exact opposite.

After a brief pause, I inquired, are you alright?" She responded, "I have had better days." It was clear that this day, was not a good day for her. At the conclusion of class she asked; "can I speak with you"? She shared with me, that her uncle had been shot and she was trying to deal with this tragedy, and wanted to stay in her dorm room. I said to her, "I am glad that you did not sit in your dorm room and you decided to come to class, this is right where you need to be." I put my arm around her as she wept, and in that moment the healing process had begun.

Sunday morning in the context of our community worship we have a moment where the entire congregation greets each other. It is a wonderful time of fellowship and in these moments I learn of many people who are going through seasons of challenge and celebration. One particular Sunday morning a member with tears in his eyes, said Pastor, I just learned that my dad passed. I stopped and put my arms around him, sharing our love and condolences. In that moment his healing had begun.

The worship continued, and we shared a wonderful experience, at the conclusion of worship I asked this grieving brother in faith, to come forward so that we the church family could pray with him. Worship provides an opportunity for healing. In the context of worship, the community can put their arms around a wounded brother and affirm Gods love, and support in the midst of grief. When we offer those who have experienced loss our presence, we are offering them Gods presence. In those moments we become the presence of God. Healing is as much about the process as the final destination. When Jesus heals there is no set prescription. Jesus heals with a word, touch and other times just Jesus' presence is enough for healing to take place.

When the Psalmist writes: "I will fear no evil for thou art with me." The psalm writer affirms I can walk through the challenges of life, why because I am not alone. The writer is saying I can handle this because God is with me. I can survive this because God is with me. On occasion I have eulogized children, leading parents through the heart breaking process of burying their child. In rooms filled with tear stained eyes and broken hearts I have sat with mothers holding their hands symbolic of God's presence.

Pain and uncertainty are all the more bearable when we do not have to bear them alone. Yes, it is so very helpful to have someone with us. It is even more helpful when that someone is God.

The heart break, illness or accident is not God's judgment. The key to surviving is faith. Faith even the size of a mustard seed, that God is with me. When we face difficult circumstances in life, the challenge is not to explain them, to justify them, or even to accept them. The challenge is to survive, walk through the valley come out on the other side and continue to live. When we choose to affirm life in the face of trail, we affirm not only that God is with us, we affirm that God is able to deliver.

**Faith in Tough Times**

We know that when we go through the wilderness, the simple profound knowledge that God is with us makes all the difference. Every person knows that when facing hardship if they have someone who will share the difficulty with them, they draw straight from each other.

One of the most challenging moments of my life was when our first son was born. It was a difficult labor for my loving wife, there was not much I could do to relieve her pain, and nevertheless I sat with her, held her hand and affirmed my love for her and our soon to be born first child. It was this psalm that anchored our faith. We knew that we were not alone. We were confident that mother, father, and baby were all in God's hands. Faith in tough times is grounded in the trust that God is with us. At times we all must pass through the wilderness of life. Just as Jesus was led by the spirit into the wilderness, so too, you and I may find ourselves being led through the wilderness.

> *1 Jesus, full of the Holy Spirit, returned from the Jordan and was led by the Spirit in the wilderness, 2 where for forty days he was tempted by the devil. He ate nothing at all during those days, and when they were over, he was famished. 3 The devil said to him, "If you are the Son of God, command this stone to become a loaf of bread." 4 Jesus answered*

*him, "It is written, one does not live by bread alone." **5** Then the devil led him up and showed him in an instant all the kingdoms of the world. **6** And the devil said to him, "To you I will give their glory and all this authority; for it has been given over to me, and I give it to anyone I please. **7** If you, then, will worship me, it will all be yours." **8** Jesus answered him, "It is written, "Worship the Lord your God, and serve only him.' "9 Then the devil took him to Jerusalem, and placed him on the pinnacle of the temple, saying to him, "If you are the Son of God, throw yourself down from here, **10** for it is written, "He will command his angels concerning you, to protect you,' **11** and "On their hands they will bear you up, so that you will not dash your foot against a stone.' "12 Jesus answered him, "It is said, "do not put the Lord your God to the test.' "13 When the devil had finished every test, he departed from him until an opportune time." (Luke 4:1-13)*

If you are facing tough times, family crisis, financial concerns, relationship upheaval, you can take strength in the promise of God, "I am with you."

Jesus was not the first person nor will he be the last in the wilderness. It is the confidence that God is with him, the certainty, "God's Spirit is on me;" Luke 4:18 (MSG) that equipped Jesus to face his wilderness experience. Jesus is our model, we make it through the challenges, and heart breaks of life, divorce, job terminations, sickness, death, we trust, moving forward, believing the promise of God's presence. God does not promise that we will not face challenges, but God's promise is that "I am with you." God will walk with you all the way through the valley and lead you to the other side. On the other side of the valley is new life. Life lived having experienced, trusted the loving presence of God.

Recently, a young woman asked me. "How do you get over a broken heart"? She continued I have just broken up with a long term relationship how long will my heart be broken? Will I ever be able to trust again? Will I be able to love again?" I shared with her, "you must be patience, do not be in a hurry. Healing is a process and healing takes time. Yes, acknowledge your broken heart. Yes, your pain is real. Give yourself time, do not pressure yourself. You will need time to trust again. You will need time to love again. Yes, you are vulnerable. You not only will survive, there will come a time when you will be able to go forward. Healing, is a process, just as we need time for physical healing we need time for spiritual and emotional healing to take place?"

I know the pain of loss. Having now buried my father and mother, I know the pain of grieving and loss. I know, of this young lady's pain of a broken heart and wondering if I will be able to be healed and go forward.

In the midst of a very challenging time in my life when my ministry was under great threat, I can remember praying and asking God what's next. I could not see even a few years ahead, I am someone who has always had the gift of vision. Vision is the ability to see a preferred tomorrow. During this uncomfortable time, I could not see, stress, pressure, hostile and a hostile environment had covered eyes. Do not look to others or the storms of life swilling around your life. Look within; God has equipped you perfectly for your journey. The treasure of the kingdom of God within is yours to claim.

The Old Testament prophet was known as the seer. Meaning that the prophet could see further down the line of time, the prophet could see what was on the horizon. When we cannot see what is ahead; this is time when we must lean on the full affirmation of the psalmist. "You are with me." I learned that even when I cannot see, God can see. I learned to trust God in the darkness. Yes, through your season of transition, you will learn to trust God.

## There Are People Who Care

When I was about ten years old, I was with my father; a strong man who believed in God but had become disillusioned with the church and her leadership. When he was a young man he witness his grandmother wounded in the context of church corruption and this failure marked his relationship with the church for the rest of his life. My brother was privilege to pray with him and help him mend a broken fence in his heart later in his life before he transitioned to be with the Lord.

The day was snowy, cold; a strong northern wind blew between the tall buildings that lined the streets of downtown Pittsburgh. I felt safe, warm, I was with my dad walking, warm coat, hat, gloves, rosy - cheeked, smiling, protected from the harsh urban environment winter day.

I notice a strange man who seemed to appear from out of nowhere, in a moment I heard him say, to my dad, "Can you help me out, can you spare some change?" My dad, instinctively, took off his gloves, reached in his pocket and handed him some money, I was certain in my child's worldview that my dad did not know the man for I had seen him do this on many occasions.

Then, my dad took his gloves, and handed them to the man. My mind even now is filled with images from that day to this, of my dad's hands, no gloves, but a warm heart.

My life was marked in a moment, a seed planted, cultivating a heart of compassion. God, was calling me to ministry, not only on Sunday morning, God was calling, teaching me Sunday's message translated to Mondays' walk. "The Word lived is an act of kindness, an act of compassion, an act of justice."

… I was hungry and you gave me food, I was thirsty and you gave me drink, I was a stranger and you welcomed me, (Matthew 25:35 RSV)

When we know people who have encountered misfortune, the best thing we can do for them is simply to be with them. We do not need to explain their suffering or try to make them feel better by telling them of people who are worse off. We do not need to defend God; God can take care of God's image. When people hurt, people need presence more than explanation. There is healing in being there, silently holding someone's hand can be a great act of healing.

When we are afflicted, this is not the time to close yourself off in a dark room, you must fight this strong temptation. You must, get yourself up, and come out of the darkness into the light. The healing light of God, walk among people, at this time in your life you need people. People sometimes say the wrong things. In their awkwardness some may even say hurtful things, you must listen behind the words and hear the message of empathy that they care for you and want to ease your pain.

As, a pastor I know this first hand. Many times good minded people in their attempt to help heal can also hurt. Words can be awkward, especially at times of loss or struggle. Yet, when we offer our presence no matter how awkward we may be, it says I recognize your suffering, we acknowledge your pain, and while I may not be able to alleviate your pain I will sit with you, that you may know that you are not alone.

## God Comforts

God appears to Moses at the Burning Bush and sends him to Pharaoh. Moses responds by asking God, "What is your name? When I go to Pharaoh and to the Israelites and tell them you sent me, and they ask me who you are, what am I to say? (Exodus 3:6-14)

In biblical times your name was more than your identification. It was your essence; it defined what you were about and what you stood for. "I am what I am." Or "I will be what I will be." This is the response of God to Moses. Two verses earlier God tells Moses, "When you go to Pharaoh, I will be with you." For me, that is God's name, the essence of what God is about. God is the one who is with us when we are tempted to feel that the universe has abandoned us. God is the one who is with us when we feel alone in the valley of the shadow of death.

Here is God saying I will be with you Moses. I will be whatever you need me to be:

I will be light in darkness.

I will be bread when you are hungry.

I will be water when you are thirsty.

I will be a bridge through the red sea.

I will be a cloud by day and fire by night.

I am that I am!

## God is with me

In the beginning God said, let there be light. Even a little bit of light is enough to dispel our fear in a room full of darkness. Like a young child who awakens in the middle of the night in total darkness, her bedroom feels like a dark empty chasm. She is frightened by the noises she hears outside, the cracking of the walls, the rattling of the windows. Yet, when the tiniest of light breaks through the darkness, she is no longer afraid. She cries out and her mother/father reassures her, her fear is dispelled. A night light is provided. Presence is now reaffirmed. She is reminded she is not alone.

Yes, God in the similar manner, when we are mired in the heaviness of life's dark midst, it takes only a ray of light to make the darkness bearable. Darkness often surrounds the light. We focus not on the darkness. We keep our eyes on the light.

I am often amazed, humbled how in a room full of crying babies a mother's ears will pick up the sound just of her crying baby. The story is told of the mother who was engrossed in a certain presentation while several babies cried in the background noise. Suddenly, the mother stopped her presentation, proceeded to say, I hear the baby crying. Those in the room said, yes you are right. The babies have been crying for some time. The mother responded, no I do not think you understand I hear my baby crying.

God is listening when we cry.

God may not change my struggle, or make my concerns disappear, yet I am certain God will be with me. It is enough to know that I am not alone. The psalmist assures me, I am not alone.

"I will fear no evil, thou art with me."

In the writing of this chapter, arriving at this point I thought the chapter was concluded. My phone just rang and it was a member of our church family who in the administrating of his profession, his life has been threatened.

**"Yea, though I walk through the valley of the shadow of death, I will hear no evil for thou art with me."**

In our conversation, which led to our praying over the phone, I prayed for Gods protection, Gods peace, and most of all God's presence. The threat of danger is all around us. Yes, we do not face danger alone. God is with us!

# CHAPTER VI

## ANOINTED AND YET STRUGGLING

*"You anoint my head with oil; my cup overflows"* (Psalm 23:5b)

As members of the household of faith, we affirm that there is one God. We who have accepted Christ Jesus as Lord, in theological context are known as monotheistic meaning we believe in one God. We affirm this one God is manifested in three distinct revelations, God the Father, God the Son, and God the Holy Spirit. (God the Father in the Old Testament, God the Son in the Gospels, and God the Holy Spirit) We now live in what is known as the age of the spirit. We use the theological word trinity to describe the unique relationship of Father, Son and Holy Spirit; we affirm that there is one God.

While Christians may disagree at times about how we discern the will of God; how we get to know God, and how we can practice the way of God. Nevertheless, we affirm as a community of faith that there is one God. One God as manifested in Christ Jesus calls us to love God, and love others.

## Anointed

In my personal journey of faith God manifests through the particular expression known as Christianity, thus I declare that I am a Christian. Meaning that by faith I have accepted Christ Jesus the anointed one into my life, that Jesus is my Lord and Savior. While I am a Christian, I am a practicing Christian. I am becoming more Christian every day. I am at peace! I seek to live in loving relationship with God and all of God's creation.

As a Christian I understand that I now live in what is called the age of the spirit. The age of the sprit is the present age now; the Holy Spirit has been released. The Holy Spirit is our dominant way of approaching God, in the age of the spirit. It is in this context, as a monotheistic person, a practicing Christian, living in the age of the spirit, who affirms that Jesus is Lord. I come to the text.

The text says, that God anoints.

*"You anoint my head with oil; my cup over flows"* (Psalm 23:5b)

By definition anoints means to pour, to smear upon. When God anoints something, an item, or somebody, it means that God has set it apart for a particular purpose or a particular mission. To anoint, meaning God has poured or smeared the spirit upon that which has been anointed. We affirm that people are set apart (anointed), for a particular function, purpose or task.

God does anoint people. We read in the scriptures that the Lord sent Samuel to anoint Saul to be King, and he anoints Saul to be King. Samuel would also anoint David to be King. Later, we read that Solomon would be anointed to be King. Both Saul and David would be set apart for a particular task or purpose. They are to be King, yet they are not yet King. God has anointed, they are to be the King, yet they must continue to grow into becoming King. Being and becoming this is the tension we live with as believers. We are saved and we are being saved.

Anointed means that God has purposed it for you, yet if you do not walk in what God has designed you have the power to circumvent what God has planned. You and I must walk in the anointing that God has purposed. We must seek to live out the anointing that God has sent.

Be careful, not to undervalue you're anointing by thinking that if I do not get paid for what I do then that must not be my anointing, how you make a living and your anointing may be two different things. Anointing, you were set apart, yet because you are anointed for a task it does not mean that you are going to get monetary compensation for it. In our world we think too often that the only things that have value are the things that we get paid for. The Job you have may not be what you are anointed for it may be given that that you can be free to do that which you have been anointed to do.

## Anointed yet Struggling

Anointed, does not mean that you will be exempt from struggle. We ask the question, how is it I must struggle when I know that I am anointed to do what I do?

David, the transitional figure between Saul and Solomon, is on his deathbed; in first Kings - David is dying. There arises in the Kingdom competing interest, rival priest each have their own candidate among David's sons to succeed him. One group anoints Solomon as the new king (while David is still alive) another anoints his brother Adonijah. One group is with Solomon and the other group is with Adonijah. It will take a deathbed intervention on Solomon's behalf to confirm him as successor.

We cannot make ourselves king, just as we cannot anoint ourselves. David gives instructions from his deathbed. That Solomon is to receive the anointing of the prophet. While Solomon is anointed there is yet struggle. God anoints, God appoints, God provides opportunity, yet we must walk in that anointing even in the midst of the struggle and opposition we will encounter. I have experienced personally the hostile environment of litigation, haivng those close to the ministry attacking my character and challenging my integrity. I never questioned my anointing even when some of those who were closest to me would do so. Anointing is a gift from God when you have it walk in it, and do not focus on those who would challenge your anointing. Stay close to God!

"You anoint my head with oil my cup overflows."

The psalmist, verse five, "you anoint my head with oil, my cup overflows." You prepare a table before me in the presence of my enemies.

Too often we associate struggle with absences of anointing. The exact opposite may be true; your anointing may be the very source of your struggle. This world can be an unfriendly place. When God sent his only begotten son, Jesus, we are clearly told, the spirit descends on him like a dove.

"9 In those days Jesus came from Nazareth of Galilee and was baptized by John in the Jordan. 10 And when he came up out of the water, immediately he saw the heavens opened and the Spirit descending upon him like a dove; 11 and a voice came from heaven, "Thou art my beloved Son; with thee I am well pleased." 12 The Spirit immediately drove him out into the wilderness. (Mark 1:9-12)

Jesus, the anointed of God yet faced challenge and struggle. The greater the anointing - the greater the struggle will be. Jesus, now being baptized by John in the river of Jordan, praying, the heavens open, the Holy Spirit descends on him like a dove, a voice from heaven: "You are my beloved son, whom I love, and am well pleased," Jesus is then led into the wilderness.

**1** Jesus, full of the Holy Spirit, returned from the Jordan and was led by the Spirit in the wilderness, **2** where for forty days he was tempted by the devil. He ate nothing at all during those days, and when they were over, he was famished. **3** The devil said to him, "If you are the Son of God, command this stone to become a loaf of bread." **4** Jesus answered him, "It is written, and "One does not live by bread alone." **5**Then the devil led him up and showed him in an instant all the kingdoms of the world. **6** And the devil said to him, "To you I will give their glory and all this authority; for it has been given over to me, and I give it to anyone I please. **7** If you, then, will worship me, it will all be yours." **8** Jesus answered him, "It is written, "Worship the Lord your God, and serve only him." **9** Then the devil took him to Jerusalem, and placed him on the pinnacle of the temple, saying to him, "If you are the Son of God, throw yourself down from here, **10** for it is written, "He will command his angels concerning you, to protect you," **11** and "On their hands they will bear you up, so that you will not dash your foot against a stone," **12** Jesus answered him, "It is said, "Do not put the Lord your God to the test." **13** When the devil had finished every test, he departed from him until an opportune time. **14** Then Jesus, filled with the power of the Spirit, returned to Galilee, and a report about him spread through all the surrounding country. **15** He began to teach in their synagogues and was praised by everyone. **16** When he came to Nazareth, where he had been brought up, he went to the synagogue on the Sabbath day, as was his custom. He stood up to read, **17** and the scroll of the prophet Isaiah was given to him. He unrolled the scroll and found the place where it was written: **18** "The Spirit of the Lord is upon me, because he has anointed me to bring good news to the poor. He has sent me to proclaim release to the captives and recovery of sight to the blind, to let the oppressed go free, **19** to proclaim the year of the Lord's favor." **Luke 4:1-19**

Jesus' journey clearly demonstrates that God's anointing will often lead to conflict with the powers of the enemy and the powers of this world.

"You anoint my head with oil."

This follows; "you prepare a table before me in the presence of my enemies."

"You anoint my head with oil."

What does this mean in the context?

"You anoint my head with oil."

**Covered**

God covers me. God pours out the spirit on me. God smears me with God's spirit. My enemies can see me, but my enemies have no power over me. They are close enough where they can see me, and I can see them. It is as if they can almost touch me. Yet, God has fixed it that my enemies are close enough to see the blessing of God in my life, but they are not so close that they can put their hands upon me. If my enemies could put their hands on me they would seek to wound me. But, God! But, God! But, God has constrained the enemy. God holds in balance my anointing and my struggle. Our anointing and our struggling are kept, in tension to remind us that it is not by our power, but by God's power, it is God who is our strength. It is God who is our help. It is God who is our keeper.

> "1 I must boast; there is nothing to be gained by it, but I will go on to visions and revelations of the Lord. 2 I know a man in Christ who fourteen years ago was caught up to the third heaven--whether in the body or out of the body I do not know, God knows. 3 And I

know that this man was caught up into Paradise-- whether in the body or out of the body I do not know, God knows-- 4 and he heard things that cannot be told, which man may not utter. 5 On behalf of this man I will boast, but on my own behalf I will not boast, except of my weaknesses. 6 Though if I wish to boast, I shall not be a fool, for I shall be speaking the truth. But I refrain from it, so that no one may think more of me than he sees in me or hears from me. 7 And to keep me from being too elated by the abundance of revelations, a thorn was given me in the flesh, a messenger of Satan, to harass me, to keep me from being too elated. 8 Three times I besought the Lord about this, that it should leave me; 9 but he said to me, "My grace is sufficient for you, for my power is made perfect in weakness." I will all the more gladly boast of my weaknesses, that the power of Christ may rest upon me. 10 For the sake of Christ, then, I am content with weaknesses, insults, hardships, persecutions, and calamities; for when I am weak, then I am strong. (2 Corinthians 12:1-10)

God's strength is made perfect in our weakness.

God has a way of keeping all things in balance. The enemy may be close, but the enemy cannot touch you, for God has you covered. Covered! God has you covered!

After twenty years of ministry at The Mount Carmel Baptist Church where I serve as Pastor, the community paused coming together with my family to celebrate the gift of God, 20 years of pastoral ministry. I shared with the church family that I felt a great sense of joy, a great sense of completion, and a great sense of purpose fulfilled. I knew in my sprit that I have been anointed and yet I have known my share of struggles.

Not only have I known struggle, I have sat with families and helped wipe tears from the eyes of those who have known the loss of loved ones as well as physical, spiritual and emotional struggle. Unexpected terminations, relationships that have been devastated under the pressure of life, others who have seen hope lost, family members lost in acts of senseless violence: yet in the mist of transition, trail and trouble God has provided.

Yes, with many other believers I can declare; "God has provided."

Yes, I can declare; "God is faithful."

Yes, God is faithful!

God has you covered!

God has you covered!

# STRENGTH

# *You Are Not Alone!*

# STRENGTH

# Chapter VII

## THE SHEPHERD'S ROD AND STAFF

Psalm 23:4 Yea, though I walk through the valley of the shadow of death, I will fear no evil for thou art with me, your Rod and Staff they comfort me.

## The Hand of God

How is it that two boys who are born in the same neighborhood one becomes a doctor and the other lies dead in a pool of blood shot in a drug deal gone bad. We hear this type of story again and again.

Is it environment?

Is it genetics?

Is it fate?

Is it destiny?

Is it the hand of God?

Life can be altered in a moment. A momentary decision can change the trajectory of our lives. A small adjustment at the beginning can change ones final outcome.

My life is a story of the improbable. I have never been arrested; I have had no addictions to drug or alcohol. My story is the exception and not the rule in the neighborhoods I grew up within. Crime and street violence were unfortunately too common. Outside of the strong commitment of loving parents, faith in God passed down from one generation to another. What were the influences that have helped to hold my life together?

I was born to a young mother and father, in an urban ghetto, my father was very intelligent but never completed the formal educational process, mine is the story of the boy who could have easily been lost to urban violence, crime or incarceration. I was blessed to have a father who loved me in my home, whereas most of the young men I grew up with did not know this privilege. I would talk with my father and he would tell me how he was raised by his grandmother. My father's grand-mother was, a tall woman, a mixture of Native American, and African American, as ironic as it sounds, whose family came out of North Carolina, and made their way to the urban center Pittsburgh Pennsylvania. When my great uncle on my father's side recently visited North Carolina, now in his eighties, he shared with me that my father's maternal side of the family came out of North Carolina, their names in the south were Robertson, and when they moved north the names became Roberts. I share the details of this story, as a reminder of what a difference a few letters can make, how small changes can make a big difference.

God is ever at work behind the curtain of time, purposes often unknown, yet the master plan of God is unfolding. I have discovered the deeper our roots the wider and stronger our branches.

We do not choose our families, yet our families mark us, the divine has connected our journey. God connects us not simply by lives of physical family bonds, but God connects us by bonds of spirit and love.

## Shepherds

Abraham, Moses, and David, were all shepherds who led God's people but they also sought to lead a family. Family, those who are closest to us; and have common world view. Those who God has connected, those who share our common story; we call family. The shepherd must lead, guide, and protect the sheep, so must the shepherd lead, guide, and protect the family.

The shepherd's staff is an enduring symbol of a shepherd's leading, guiding, and protecting the sheep. It is used to nudge newborn sheep to their mother, guide sheep through a maze of trails, and protect them from enemies that lie in wait. Ancient kings used the staff as a symbol of their just and compassionate rule. It is a fitting icon for a spiritual shepherd who leads God's flock. The staff is also a wonderful symbol for a father or mother seeking to lead a family.

On the occasion of two of our young ministers graduating from seminary, they presented me with a wonderful gift of a shepherd's staff. The staff they presented was a symbol of the leadership, guidance, and yes protection. When I go into my office, there the pastor's staff rest as an ever reminder of my responsibility to lead, guide, and protect the community, the household of faith, as well as my nuclear family. The shepherd must model and protect the unity of the faith and family.

**Lean on God**

One of the functions of the shepherd's staff was for it to be an instrument designed to help hold the shepherd up. The shepherd understood that even when he was by himself he could lean on God. The staff is the symbol of a strong God that we can lean on.

The matriarch of our family was my grandmother. My grandmother like many of the senior women in the community was our spiritual as well as physical anchor. Although she has gone on to be with the Lord, her life lessons influence and yet speak from the galleries of glory. I watched her with grace nurture four generations, ever affirming her strength which came from her confidence in knowing that she could lean on the Lord.

With great skill and her own unique logistical system, my grandmother was able to communicate with her many grand and great grandchildren. She was the hub of our family, keeping track of birthdays, communicating who was sick, and who was facing challenges. When her children and grandchildren began to move from our hometown, it was her wisdom that we would seek if we needed another family member's contact information. She was our information system.

Yes, we came to learn over time that we could lean on her. It was not until she passed that we all realized how much we leaned on her to keep us all together.

The staff is a symbol that we can lean on God who keeps us together. Just as the shepherd leans on the staff, symbolic of the shepherd leaning on God, the sheep lean on the shepherd, and the shepherd leans on God. Know today that you can lean on God.

**God Guides**

The second purpose of the rod and staff is to be a symbol that God will guide your steps. The rod becomes an instrument of direction and guidance.

Read again, the early part of psalms 23:

"He maketh me to lie down in green pastures.

He leadeth me beside the still waters

He restores my soul."

God will lead the community, and God will lead the family. We have all heard it said; "the family that prays together stays together". Prayer is the gift of God. Prayer is loving, honest communication with God. What is needed in prayer is an open heart. The key is not eloquence of word, or the recitation of creed. Whatever your struggles, trouble or trials God is available. I am certain that prayer is one of Gods greatest gift. Like any gift prayer must be opened, received and utilized for it to be effect.

God will direct, and God will guide. My life is a story of the guiding hand of God. My story is the story of a boy born into urban poverty, whose early years nurtured in the crucible of the black church tradition. Public schools, state university, seminary, family conversations over the dinner table, urban black church, the strong tradition of rising above poverty, and oppression, God was ever at work. I realize that my life is the dream of grandparents and parents who believed that God would guide and God would protect.

When the disciples were seeking God's guidance having observed Jesus, who had declared, "I do nothing on my own," the disciples seeking the guidance of God, noticed that Jesus would retreat in prayer. The prayer life of Jesus was of such maturity, that the disciples asked Jesus, "Teach us to pray!" Jesus response:

"Pray then like this. Our Father who art in heaven. Hallowed be thy name. Thy Kingdom come. Thy will be done. On earth as it is in heaven. Give us this day our daily bread. And forgive us our debts. As we also have forgiven our debtors. And lead us not into temptation. But deliver us from evil. (Mathew 6:9-13)

Here is the petition for spiritual as well as physical daily guidance. Daily bread is the expression that the disciple leans on the Lord for guidance. Daily prayer is the expression that no matter what the circumstance, you can lean on God. Daily bread is the expression of the humblest of resource and substance; in every need you can lean on God.

## God Provides

Young sheep know that as long as the shepherd is watching, they are guided, protected, and comforted. When we know that somebody is watching out for us, we develop a new confidence and strength. When we are loved, loved by the shepherd it provides a strength that is unspeakable. The shepherd ever ready protecting the sheep that rest under the shepherd stewardship. As the father watches over his children, so God watches over God's children.

**1** Now all the tax collectors and sinners were coming near to listen to him. **2** And the Pharisees and the scribes were grumbling and saying, "This fellow welcomes sinners and eats with them." **3**So he told them this parable: **4** "Which one of you, having a hundred sheep and losing one of them, does not leave the ninety-nine in the wilderness and go after the one that is lost until he finds it? **5** When he has found it, he lays it on his shoulders and rejoices. **6** And when he comes home, he calls together his friends and neighbors, saying to them, "Rejoice with me, for I have found my sheep that was lost.' **7** Just so, I tell you, there will be more joy in heaven over one sinner who repents than over ninety-nine righteous persons who need no repentance. **8** "Or what woman having ten silver coins, if she loses one of them, does not light a lamp, sweep the house, and search carefully until she finds it? **9** When she has found it, she calls together her friends and neighbors, saying, "Rejoice with me, for I have found the coin that I had lost.' **10** Just so, I tell you, there is joy in the presence of the angels of God over one sinner who repents." **11** Then Jesus said, "There was a man who had two sons. **12** The younger of them said to his father, "Father, give me the share of the property that will belong to me.' So he divided his property between them.**13** A few days later the younger son gathered all he had and traveled to a distant country, and there he squandered his property in dissolute living. **14** When he had spent everything, a severe famine took place throughout that country, and he began to be in need. **15** So he went and hired himself out to one of the citizens of that country, who sent him to his fields to feed the pigs. **16** He would gladly have filled himself with the pods that the pigs were eating; and no one gave him anything. **17** But when he came to himself he said, "How many of my father's hired hands have bread enough and to spare, but here I am dying of hunger! **18** I will get up and go to my father, and I will say to him, "Father, I have sinned against heaven and before you; **19** I am no longer worthy to be called your son; treat me like one of your hired hands." '20 So he set off and went to his father. But while he was still far off, his father saw him and was filled with compassion; he ran and put his arms around him and kissed him. **21** Then the son said to him, "Father, I have sinned against heaven and before you; I am no longer worthy to be called your son.' **22** But the father said to his slaves, "Quickly, bring out a robe—the best one—and put it on him; put a ring on his finger and sandals on his feet. **23** And get the fatted calf and kill it, and let us eat and celebrate; **24** for this son of mine was dead and is alive again; he was lost and is found!' And they began to celebrate. (Luke 15:1-24)

Here is a wonderful story of a lost sheep, a lost coin, and a lost boy. God's willingness to bring that which is lost safely home:

**A lost sheep:** The shepherd who has ninety-nine sheep safe in the fold is willing to go out in search of the lost one. When the shepherd has found it, he lays it on his shoulders and rejoices. And when he comes home, he calls together his friends and neighbors, saying to them, "Rejoice with me, for I have found my sheep that was lost."

**A lost coin:** A woman having ten silver coins, if she loses one of them, lights a lamp, sweep the house, and search carefully until she finds it? When she has found it, she calls together her friends and neighbors, saying, "Rejoice with me, for I have found the coin that I had lost."

**A lost boy:** The father, when the boy comes home, bring out a robe—the best one—and put it on him; put a ring on his finger and sandals on his feet. Get the fatted calf and kill it, and let us eat and celebrate; "for this son of mine was dead and is alive again; he was lost and is found!' Let the celebration begin.

We celebrate God who loves us enough to rejoice when we make our way home. Let none of us ever declare I found the Lord. We can never find the Lord, for he is ever watching, searching, waiting for us to come to understand that it is God who asks, "Adam, where are you?" God is giving us the opportunity to come back home. Home is wherever God is at. "Your rod and staff they comfort me!"

Come Home Today!

Let the Celebration begin!

# STRENGTH

# Chapter VIII

# MY CUP OVERFLOWS

"Thou preparest a table before me in the presence of my enemies; thou anointest my head with oil, my cup overflows." Psalm 23:5

## Say Thank You

My great grandmother Mrs. Cora Lee Weatherly was a kind and endearing woman who believed in the goodness of the Lord in the land of the living. While she lived in the urban north she was of that generation who made the pilgrimage from the south to the north in search of a better life. I find it ironic that three generations later I like many in my generation have made that same journey only in reverse moving from the north to the south. Solomon got it right there is nothing new under the sun. Mrs. Cora Lee Weatherly left me with many life lessons, and chief among those life lessons was the simple act of saying thank you. She was of a generation that the smallest act of kindness warranted authentic expression of appreciation. Hers was a generation where gratitude and graciousness were seen as a way of life. This attitude of gratitude flowed from a deep reservoir of faith in a God who was gracious even in the most difficult of times.

She understood that to be gracious did not change the sometimes difficult reality that she faced, but graciousness did have the power to make the journey of life sweeter.

Yes, God did send the rain on the just and the unjust. The rain was necessary that God might grow the fruit of life. In her mind's eye the very food that she ate was a gift, the fruit of a gracious God. Thus, the only appropriate response to life was gratitude. Gratitude, defined as the simple expression of saying thank you. Too say, thank you, is to recognize that God created the world, and all that we know comes from the hand of God. It is not my world, it is God's world, and when I look around and witness the miracle of life, I declare: "the earth is the Lord's and the fullness thereof."

Remember the ten lepers that Jesus healed:

> **12** As he entered a village, ten lepers approached him. Keeping their distance, **13** they called out, saying, "Jesus, Master, have mercy on us!" **14** When he saw them, he said to them, "Go and show yourselves to the priests." And as they went, they were made clean. **15** Then one of them, when he saw that he was healed, turned back, praising God with a loud voice. **16** He prostrated himself at Jesus' feet and thanked him. And he was a

Samaritan. **17** Then Jesus asked, "Were not ten made clean? But the other nine, where are they? **18** Was none of them found to return and give praise to God except this foreigner?" **19** Then he said to him, "Get up and go on your way; your faith has made you well." Luke 17:12-19

Say Thank you!

## Somebody Who Loves You

The lesson of gratitude that my great grandmother shared with me flowed out of the stream of love. I count her love as one of the great gifts of God in my life. The love of a great grandmother, mother, and now a loving wife, has been by far the sweetest gifts of God I have ever known. I consider my life blessed having known and received the gift of a love. When I think of the love of God, the closest experience that I can relate is that of a loving mother. In the Bible the primary motif of God is that of a loving father, "when you pray say Our Father who art in heaven." Jesus clearly understood the unique love of a mother. At cavalry's cross, Jesus looked upon his mother Mary and John the beloved disciple and when Jesus saw his mother and the disciple whom he loved standing beside her, he said to his mother, "Woman, here is your son." (Luke 19:26)

If you have been given the gift of love in this world, be certain to stop and say "thank you." I can think of no other gift that holds more value than the gift of love. God gives his only begotten son, as a demonstration of God's great love. "For God so loved the world that he gave his only begotten son, that whoever believes in him should not perish but have eternal life. "(John 3:16)

Gratitude is not simply a process of receiving. Gratitude is a reciprocal process. It is the act of giving and receiving. When we accept a gift, we say thank you. We bless the giver with our appreciation, even as the giver has blessed us with their kindness. A life of gratitude is maturing to the place of awareness. I am a receiver of gifts, yet as well I must be a gift giver. God gave us the gift of his son Jesus. When we receive the gift of God into our lives, we now become heirs to the Kingdom of God. Every good and perfect gift comes from above. Jesus is God's gift of love. Say Thank You!

## Life Is a Gift

Life is a gift. God is the giver of the gift. We bless God with appreciation for the gift. A young child comes with a gift, and presents it to her mother. The mother receives the gift. The mother is excited, overcome with a feeling of joy. The mother knows that the young child has no money to buy the gift. Mother knows the young child had to get the money from someone else, but this does not steal her joy for what she celebrates is the extending of love that the child has shown. The value of the gift is of no consequence. The gift is not simply the item shared, but the priceless gift of being loved.

Every Sunday is God's mother's day. Every Sunday when we worship the Lord we bring ourselves into worship in the context of the church community, we present our lives as gifts to the Lord. We are saying thank you God for the gift of life. God receives the presentations of our lives with gratitude. We are saying thank you to God, and God is saying thank you to us. Say Thank you!

**Why Can't I Say Thank You**

Why is it then so difficult, for many people to say thank you. It sounds so simple, yet it can be very difficult. Just to say thank you. I call this a theology of "I can't." Meaning I can't say thank you, because I have no reason to say thank you. It is the view of life, which declares; "I can do it on my own. I don't need anyone else." This finds its expression in phrases like, "I am a self-made man/woman. I can make it on my own." This theology of "I can't" must be replaced with a theology of "I can."

"I can." Because I am created in the image of God, "I can give and I can receive." I can because I understand that I am connected. Connected to God, and connected to others. My connection is not weakness, but this is my strength.

Here in the 23rd psalm the psalmist allows us to peer into the inner recess of mind and spirit. Writing and giving us hints that life is not always easy.

"Even though I walk through the valley of the shadow of death, I fear no evil; for thou art with me; thy rod and thy staff, they comfort me. Thou preparest a table before me in the presence of my enemies; thou anointest my head with oil, my cup overflows." Life has had its share of challenges:

"Yea, though I walk through the valley of the shadow of death, I will fear no evil." "Thou preparest a table before me in the presence of my enemies."

In order to have a table prepared in the presence of my enemies, I must have enemies. While very few would choose to have enemies, life has a way of bringing to us those who would oppose our hopes and dreams. I heard a wonderful sermon preached some years ago on this very subject. The focus of the sermon was let God take care of your enemies and you keep your eye on the table. The table is the place where God is providing your blessing.

I would like to take that a little further, keep your eyes on the table. On the table God has prepared your blessing. On the table rest your cup. The proclamation of the 23rd psalm is, "my cup overflows," "my cup runneth over." The psalmist understands that we will face challenges, and difficulties. Yet the psalmist does not suggest that we will be unable to deal with these situations. The writer exudes a spiritual confidence that declares. "I trust God."

"I can trust."

"I will trust God."

It is out of my confidence in a loving God that I can say. "Thank you!"

Say Thank you!

## My Cup Runs Over

Here is a simple expression that God's capacity of generosity is much larger that our capacity to contain what God pours into our lives. In short, the cup is not large enough to hold God's capacity to give. The church of my youth was fond of saying, "you can't beat God giving." Even if I get a larger cup (bucket size) God's capacity to pour out the blessing is yet still larger than my cup.

In the cup I see references of faith. My faith has to continue to enlarge that I might receive an overflowing blessing. I must allow my faith to expand to be drawn closer to God. I am not overly concerned with the size if someone else's cup. What God has for me is for me. God not only fills my cup, but all who have been invited to the table. I rejoice with my sisters and brothers when God bless' them. The blessing is the act of a gracious God. A gracious God who calls me to live a gracious life, life is not self-centered but God-centered. At my core is a spirit of thanksgiving. At my core is a spirit of celebration.

So, what do I do!

I Say thank you!

I live out thank you!

I live with a gracious spirit!

I live with a humble spirit!

I thank God for the gift of love!

I celebrate the relationships in my life!

Every day is a day of thanksgiving!

I come into the house of the Lord!

I come with praise and thanksgiving on my lip and in my heart!

David got it right:

"Thou preparest a table before me in the presence of my enemies; thou anointest my head with oil, my cup overflows."

Say Thank you!

Say Thank you!

Thank you Father…

Thank you Father…

# CHAPTER IX

# AN OPEN HAND AND A LOVING HEART

Surely goodness and mercy shall follow me all the days of my life, and I shall dwell in the house of the Lord my whole life long. Psalm 23:6

## Introduction

When the psalmist writes "surely goodness and mercy shall follow me all the days of my life," the writer is expressing in prayer language a certain confidence that is born out of the journey of life. The 23rd psalm perhaps one of the most beloved and endearing scriptures to ever be read or recited, in my spirit is a living prayer.

### Living Prayer

Living prayer, here the writer is expressing confidence in God. The psalm writer has an unquestionable, indisputable, certainty; without doubt he echoes through time; "surely goodness and mercy will follow me all the days of my life."

This is not a prayer similar to Psalm 120 *"In my distress I cry to the Lord, that he may answer me:" (Psalm 120:1)*

Here there is no hint that the Lord will not answer. Here is a certainty, with bold confidence, an uncanny kind of sagacity that makes religious people nervous. Faith ought to give you confidence. You ought not to walk through life timid at every turn. Sometimes you ought to tell the adversary, run. Too many people of faith are timid these days; they seem to have so much uncertainty in what they can believe. There is no uncertainty here.

> **Psalm 23:6** *Surely goodness and mercy shall follow me all the days of my life, and I shall dwell in the house of the Lord my whole life long.*
> *The psalmist is certain; there is a certain confidence that ought to come with faith.*

In that certainty the psalmist is confident that God will provide. God will provide a very certain blessing. With caution, I say blessings, because too often when I say blessings too many of us think material blessings. Many think blessings are simply about things. Yet, the psalmist talks of a certainty of blessing that is very clear. The psalmist says, he will be blessed, and the blessing is God.

The psalmist has a certainty that he can count and affirm Gods love. His confidence is born not out of his own substance, or his own capacity. It is not born out of who he is; it is born out of who God is. My confidence in God is not based on me, I am feeble and weak-kneed. My confidence in

God is based on God who is strong. The psalmist says, not maybe, but surly goodness and mercy will follow me all the days of my life.

So, then what is the blessing that this psalmist is so confident that God will provide. Very simply the blessing is The Lord God; do not sleep on that - here is the key to this sermonic moment. The psalmist will be blessed, and the blessing is God, God's love! The psalmist will be blessed with God's love, how is this possible - not because of who he the psalmist is, but because of who God is.

The psalmist is confident, "surely, goodness and mercy shall follow me.

Note, that this is verse six. This is the last verse of the psalm

This comes after:

**4** Yea, though I walk through the valley of the shadow of death,
After, I will fear no evil: for thou art with me; thy rod and thy staff they comfort me.
After affirming, **5** Thou prepares a table before me in the presence of mine enemies:
After, thou anoint my head with oil; my cup runneth over.

Then with confidence:

**6** Surely goodness and mercy shall follow me all the days of my life: and I will dwell in the house of the LORD forever.

## Goodness and Mercy

Here is why this psalm speaks to so many of us. It is not simply about getting to heaven. So many people are preoccupied with getting to heaven, their souls are trapped, living hopeless, loveless, joyless; their hope is in dying. The psalmist' affirmation is I do not have to die to experience the goodness and mercy of God. He says that goodness and mercy will follow me all the days of my life. I do not have to die for God to take care of me.

Here are two wonderful words; goodness and mercy. For the psalmist, goodness and mercy clearly go together. It is intentional that he phrases these two together. Now, we have to be careful because they are not synonymous. They do not mean the exact same thing but they belong together.

Goodness is the open hand of God.

Mercy is the heart of God.

Goodness is that God comes to me with an open hand.

Mercy is God's open hand that flows out of the heart of God.

When the psalmist says goodness and mercy, he is saying that God comes to me not with sword to wound. God comes with open hand and loving heart. Mercy here in its original Hebrew is "hesed" "loving kindness the heart of God."

Mercy is received; we have not earned and may not deserve mercy. Mercy is "hesed" loving kindness.

## Loving Kindness

I grew up in a large extended family, in one of those families, where aunts and uncles were so close that their children played together like sisters and brothers. It was in the innocence of child play I experienced loving kindness. I remember ever so vividly, the sounds, smells, and images of My aunts' home a place where community was created; laughter, struggle mixed in a cacophony of life as cousins struggle to mark their place in the family.

I remember these moments as the experience of love. Love, was no distance psychological phrase, no, love was practical, love was tangible, love was a warm place, on a cold afternoon hot soup and a well place sandwich. Love was discovering the world a rich and diverse place, where we learned that more than your own needs must be considered. Love was an act of kindness in the mist of daily challenge.

Yes, Paul did get this right. "Though I speak with the tongues of men and angels, but have not love, I have become as sounding brass or clanging cymbal." (1 Cor. 13:1)

A beautiful biblical image of love kindness is in the prophet Hosea chapter one.

*Hosea 1:1 The word of the LORD that came to Hose'a the son of Be-e'ri, in the days of Uzzi'ah,*

*Jotham, Ahaz, and Hezeki'ah, kings of Judah, and in the days of Jerobo'am the son of Jo'ash, king of Israel. 2 When the LORD first spoke through Hose'a, the LORD said to Hose'a, "Go, take to yourself a wife of harlotry and have children of harlotry, for the land commits great harlotry by forsaking the LORD." 3 So he went and took Gomer the daughter of Dibla'im, and she conceived and bore him a son.*

Here is a parable story of how Israel has forsaken God. When we get to Hosea the second chapter, verse nineteen, we are read:

Hosea 2:19 And I will take you for my wife forever; I will take you for my wife in righteousness and in justice, in steadfast love, and in mercy. 20 I will take you for my wife in faithfulness; and you shall know the Lord. 21 On that day I will answer, says the Lord, I will answer the heavens and they shall answer the earth; 22 and the earth shall answer the grain, the wine, and the oil, and they shall answer Jezreel; 23 and I will sow him for myself in the land. And I will have pity on Lo-ruhamah, and I will say to Lo-ammi, "You are my people"; and he shall say, "You are my God."

When the psalmist says surely goodness and mercy shall follow me all the days of my life, he has come to learn that he belongs to God. Yahweh is his God. Now there are certain characteristics about Yahweh we must understand. When the psalmist says surely goodness and mercy will follow me, he is saying not only will it follow me, it will pursue me, it will track me down. I cannot hide, if I go into the cave, goodness and mercy will come and find me in the cave. Surely, goodness and mercy will find me.

If I go hide in the drug house, God will see me, God will come into the drug house. When I am trying to do everything I think that I am old enough to do, I cannot get away from God, because I belong to God. God will track me down. Goodness and mercy will track me down, reminding me that I am a child of God.

We think that when we sin, because we fall from God, that God will not come and find us. God will come and find us in a ditch or in a pig's pen. God will make that ditch uncomfortable. Until we fall on our knees, declaring, "Lord has mercy on me!" God will not leave us alone until we make our way back into the fold of God. We cannot find enough mud to hide from God. We cannot rest in our sin.

It is the Hosea story over and over again. "I love you." The promise of my blessing to you is I will keep on loving. Go wandering in the street, fall down in the mud, in a pig's pen, I will keep loving you. I have called you. I am drawing you unto my love. You are my child. I will never stop loving you.

I give you the certainty of my blessing, "hesed" unmerited love. I will keep on loving you even if you will not love me back. If you run away from home, if you are lost in the darkness I will keep on loving you.

One writer said it this way;

**1 Corinthians 13:1** If I speak in the tongues of mortals and of angels, but do not have love, I am a noisy gong or a clanging cymbal. **2** And if I have prophetic powers, and understand all mysteries and all knowledge, and if I have all faith, so as to remove mountains, but do not have love, I am nothing. **3** If I give away all my possessions, and if I hand over my body so that I may boast, but do not have love, I gain nothing. **4** Love is patient; love is kind; love is not envious or boastful or arrogant **5** or rude. It does not insist on its own way; it is not irritable or resentful; **6** it does not rejoice in wrongdoing, but rejoices in the truth. **7** It bears all things, believes all things, hopes all things, and endures all things. **8** Love never ends. But as for prophecies, they will come to an end; as for tongues, they will cease; as for knowledge, it will come to an end. **9** For we know only in part, and we prophesy only in part; **10** but when the complete comes, the partial will come to an end. **11** When I was a child, I spoke like a child, I thought like a child, I reasoned like a child; when I became an adult, I put an end to childish ways. **12** For now we see in a mirror, dimly, but then we will see face to face. Now I know only in part; then I will know fully, even as I have been fully known. **13** And now faith, hope, and love abide, these three; and the greatest of these is love.

## All the Days of My Life

I was praying over this word, and the spirit revealed a new lesson. "Surely goodness and mercy shall follow me all the days of my life." In my study I discovered goodness was the open hand of God, and mercy was a loving heart. Next, I understood that God pursues me. Why then is God pursuing me? Why are you, God, tracking me down? I heard God saying yes, I am pursuing you, so that you will experience love, love comes through us, but love does not come from us. We are a conduit of love; God is the originator of love. "God is Love." (1 John 4:8)

**Revelations 22:1** Then he showed me the river of the water of life, bright as crystal, flowing from the throne of God and of the Lamb **2** through the middle of the street of the city…
What a wonderful image of God's love flowing through the city.

I love my children!

I love my children, anything I have they have.

I have food, they have food.

I have a house, they have a house.

I have money, they have money.

I have a table, they have a table.

God loves me and God is my father.

Then whatever God has I have.

God has food, and then I have food.

Whatever Gods has, I have.

Not because God gives me things, but because God gives me God's Love.

God's Love is everything.

"Surely goodness and Mercy will follow me all the days of my life."

# CHAPTER X

## The Most Comforting Words Ever

"And I shall dwell in the house of the Lord forever"

## The Gift of a Brother

One of the most formative relationships in my life has been my relationship with my older brother. In my mind's eye he has been that person who has always been there. In the early moments of consciousness, in the formative years of my life I most often saw my life as a reflection of my older brother.

I am not sure if all siblings experience this, but my big brother, as I would call him in my youth, was almost two years older than me. Just enough so that he was always a step ahead of me, but never so far out in front that I did not seek with vigor to catch up with him. Many of the lessons I learned in my youth were the result of his love, care, and sometimes not so gentle guidance.

My brother, has been for me a constant rock, and as an older sibling has always demonstrated a deep concern for my welfare, and been a caregiver both distant and near. My mother would tell the story of how it was my brother who taught me to tie my shoes, or how when I was born he would stand over me and say "my baby".

127

In our adult years I have sought to be a greater support to him, because in the back of my mind I sense he has poured far more into my life than I will ever be able to share. My older brother has been a symbol of safety and security. Both our parents now having transitioned to be with the Lord, thus, he and I alone remain to be able to tell the story of our childhood, family, and common story.

I have sat with many persons who have lost those who are closest to them; parents, siblings, children and so often they will ask, "how long will I feel like this, how long will this be with me?" I remind them that the loss of a loved one is a process, and it will take time for God's healing. Yet, even with God's healing I have discovered that the loss we experience of loved ones will always be with us. This type of loss draws us closer to God.

## The Psalmist

The psalmist affirms that he is safe and secure, he gives thanks to God. God is like the faithful shepherd who provides and protects.

The Lord is my shepherd, I shall not want

He makes me to lie down in green pastures,

He leads me beside the still waters.

He restores my souls.

He guides me in the right paths for his names sake,

Here in this initial offering of faith, the psalmist demonstrates a confidence that cannot be shaken.

"The Lord is my shepherd."

I have found that if we can offer no other words of comfort these words are always appropriate. I have sat with persons who have been so broken along their earth journey that they have not been able to get past the first verse.

"The Lord is my shepherd."

When we face life's most difficult moments, it is okay to just stay right there.

"The Lord is my shepherd."

When we are ill-equipped spiritually, emotionally, mentally, to be able to face the challenges before us, it is our confidence in God that allows us to hold on.

When the psalmist life is interrupted by trauma, tragedy, and bereavement, and the lush green pastures and still waters have all gone by the way side; when the writer finds he is alone in a dark valley, it is the relationship that has been forged with the Lord across the years that holds.

Yea, though I walk through the valley of the shadow of death.

I will fear evil.

The green pastures have turned to dark valleys. God is with him, and God is there to comfort him. Yet, the psalmist is aware: he is not alone.

## The Most Comforting Word Ever

These are the most comforting words I have ever heard.

For thou art with me.

Thy rod and Thy staff, they comfort me.

Thou preparest a table before me in the presence of mine enemies.

Thou anointest my head with oil.

My cup runneth over.

Maturing faith understands not only is the psalmist not alone, God gives the great invitation. God is not one who just follows him through the trauma, or tragedy. But, God now offers him a permanent relationship, and invitation to dwell in Gods House.

And I shall dwell in the House of the Lord forever.

And I shall dwell in the House of the Lord forever.

The psalmist, having affirmed all that God has done for him has saved the best for last. God, who provides, God who stills the ragging storm, God who leads him through the valley of the shadow of death, and then God gives the most spectacular gift that one can give: God invites the writer, the psalmist, into the gift of God's presence, into the house of the lord, to be loved all the days of his life. The psalmist affirms with confidence, "and I shall dwell in the house of the Lord (forever) my whole life long."

Here is the work of God. God is not leading us to success, whatever that envisioning may be. God is not interested in making us successful as defined by the powers of this world. God is interested in a loving relationship that glorifies God. The church fathers said it this way, "the chief end of man was to glorify God."

God is interested in redeeming that which was lost. We are at our best when we are simply being. Being what God has created us to be, the glorification of God.

It is at this point that we stop trying to live, and are alive. Alive, knowing that I am a child of God; I am not waiting to become God's child. God's perfect work is already at work in me. I am not trying, to become – so many still waiting on their promise – my promise is here, just as Judas misunderstood what it meant for Jesus to be King, Messiah. Many today misunderstand what it means to inherit God's kingdom.

"And I shall dwell in the house of the Lord my whole life long." This is the promise of God. This is what God desires for you, God is interested in relationship not ownership. Love that is built on possessions, control, and power is not love at all. When the control runs out, we are left empty and wanting. God is Love, thus Love is God.

Our faith is not rules creeds or principles; our faith is about relationship, the invitation of our Lord is not to master the Ten Commandments, not to memorize the creeds of church fathers or even to live by a set of Christian principles. Our invitation is to enter into a loving relationship with the Lord Jesus Christ.

The challenge of faith is not necessary to learn something new. The challenge of faith most often is to unlearn those habits and thinking that hinder us from childlike faith.

> Matthew 18:1-5 At that time the disciples came to Jesus, saying, "Who is the greatest in the kingdom of heaven?" 2 And calling to him a child, he put him in the midst of them, 3 and said, "Truly, I say to you, unless you turn and become like children, you will never enter the kingdom of heaven. 4 Whoever humbles himself like this child, he is the greatest in the kingdom of heaven. 5 "Whoever receives one such child in my name receives me;

> Surely goodness and mercy shall follow me all the days of my life,

> **And I shall dwell in the House of the Lord forever.**

> When we read in Matthew 5:3-8
> 3 "Blessed are the poor in spirit, for theirs is the kingdom of heaven.
> 4 "Blessed are those who mourn, for they shall be comforted.
> 5 "Blessed are the meek, for they shall inherit the earth.
> 6 "Blessed are those who hunger and thirst for righteousness, for they shall be satisfied.

**7** "Blessed are the merciful, for they shall obtain mercy.
**8** "Blessed are the pure in heart, for they shall see God.

The beatitudes are not a set of rules, creeds or principles to live by, but here is a state of being. Become the faith. Become the love of Christ. Become the peace of God.

When we fall in Love with this God manifested in The Christ Jesus, our love will bridge the gaps of our weakness, and we will day by day become more of what Christ Jesus imagined for our life. You will be blessed.

It is in this state that one lives, dwell in the house of the Lord, all the days of my life. In this state of being, we are alive.

We live seeking not simply a promise of life after physical death, we live daily experiencing the promise of life. Jesus departing the earthly realm prepares his disciples to continue living.

Matthew 28:18 And Jesus came and said to them, "All authority in heaven and on earth has been given to me. 19 Go therefore and make disciples of all nations, baptizing them in the name of the Father and of the Son and of the Holy Spirit, 20 teaching them to observe all that I have commanded you; and lo, I am with you always, to the close of the age."

I must confess that when I read this my thoughts run to the other world. But, this is a promise for this world, the promise of God's presence.

"I will be with you."

And I shall dwell in the House of the Lord forever.

Can we imagine for a moment.

God's house.

God's house.

To dwell in all the days of my life.

God's house is a sanctuary in the sense of a holy place (Sanctus means holy.)

God's house is the physical representation of an invisible God.

## Adam and Eve

Recall, Adam and Eve in the Garden of Eden, before Adam and Eve ate the forbidden fruit, they are described as "naked but feeling no shame" (Genesis 2:25). After they eat of the tree of knowledge they realize they are naked, and tried to hide from God.

Prior to the fall they live in the presence of God, no shame, no condemnation. Dare I suggest that it was their new realization of separation from God that caused them to be ashamed? Nakedness is not simply a physical condition;

we are naked when we are out of the will, the presence of God. When we are naked not covered by the Holy Spirit, we know instinctively that we are vulnerable. Without God's presence we all experience a sense of aloneness, incompleteness.

Here is where we witness Gods creativity. God created Eve and Adam as mates declaring, "It is not good for man to be alone"

"It is not good for any of us to be alone.

We must stay connected.

We must stay connected.

We must stay connected with God and we must stay connected with each other.

We too often desire to fill that void, the void of disconnection.

Work will not suffice.

Play will not suffice.

Ego will not suffice.

Power will not suffice.

Wealth will not suffice.

Can you not hear that old song?

What can wash away my sins nothing but the blood of Jesus?

What can make me whole again nothing but the blood of Jesus?

Oh, precious is the flow that makes we white as soon, no other fountain I know, nothing but the blood of Jesus.

I shall dwell in the House of the Lord forever.

I shall dwell in the House of the Lord forever.

I shall dwell in the House of the Lord forever.

I shall dwell in the House of the Lord forever.

The 23rd psalm is simply the most comforting words ever. In September of 2012, I was talking with my dear friend and sister, Pastor Miller. We were sharing some of the items we were working on, while encouraging one another. In the mist of the conversation she said to me, "I am glad you are back". Our phone conversation concluded and I thought no more concerning those remarks.

The next day, those words were quickening in my spirit. "I am glad you are back." In that moment I understood what she meant. Let, me explain. Earlier that year my mother passed, and I went through the grieving process privately and publically; I soon came realize that I was unwilling to talk about this experience publically. In truth when my mother died something in me died. The story of my childhood that can only be uniquely shared between a mother and child died. The lessons of my youth learned from the mind and heart of my mother, no other in this world could I share.

Every Sunday, I would stand before the people of faith and share in the teaching and preaching ministry the "Word of God". I was keenly aware, the people had not come to commensurate my life journey, nor to witness my pain from week to week. The people gathered to worship the Lord, bringing their trials, troubles, hurts and heart breaks, they had come to experience the Word of Life, Hope, Joy and Love.

Yet, what happens when the pastor is mourning. Yes, my faith was strong. I was certain that where ever heaven was (God's perfect presence) my mother resided with God. My unwillingness to talk about her death publically was a manifestation of my true pain, and my broken heart. Grieving is a season of life. I had been grieving! The process of grief goes on for a very long time. For years, not days or months, a parent, child, or a spouse; some lose we will carry with us all our lives. My season of grieving had been nine months. Grieving not only for the loss of my mother, but I would come to realize that something inside of me had died. I remember the first moments when I was able to speak her name publically without tears streaming from my eyes. "I was at last back!"

God gave me the strength to be able to walk back from the valley of the shadow of death. My strength was in rediscovering in the 23 psalm. God lead me back!

Back meant for me, that I was ALIVE! Yes, I miss her every day of my life. She is and every will be a part of the very fabric of my daily living. Yet, I am alive, to the place of light in the mist of the valley of darkness. I am alive, to being able to talk about my mother and be at peace. I am alive, going past the surface of thought now willing to engage in conversation concerning the depth of God. I am alive, writing which is the true sign that 'I am healed". I have written this book out of the great love for my mother Delberta Kelly Jones Kimbrough. Her unceasing love, willingness to invest her life in the lives of her two boys, Archie and Casey can never be repaid. Like all she had her struggles, her own weakness, but it is her STRENGHT that I choose to remember. Rev. Delberta J. Kimbrough was the strongest women I have ever met. She was clear that that her strength came for the Lord. Her life will always serve for me as an instrument of strength and inspiration.

I do not know how long it will take for you to come through your pain. Yet, I can affirm that you will come through. Yes, God is faithful. God has given the greatest gift of eternity. God has given us the gift of love, the gift and miracle of Gods' only begotten son, Jesus.

"For God so loved the world that he gave his only begotten son that whoever believes on him should not perish but have ever lasting life." (John 3:16)

You will know that you are alive, when your heart, mind, soul, and strength release your spirit. Your spirit will flow like rivers of water. In this place your will breathe deeply without fear, worry, anxiety or heart break. The birds will sound sweeter. The sun will shine brighter. The wind will smell fresher. You will know that life is a gift, that life is to be celebrated ever day. The spirit of thanksgiving will claim your soul. You will sing a new song. You will declare with all the cosmic order; **"I AM ALIVE!"**

**ALIVE!**

**ALIVE!**

**Jesus is the way back.**

Travel with Jesus; on the way, the process evolves:

**Daily prayer,**

**Bible study,**

**Worship,**

**Share,**

**Serve,**

**And most of all keep Loving God,**

**And keep loving others.**

Today, I pray for you.

Today, I Love you.

Today my meditation is; "God help all those who are trying to get back.

Today my meditation is; "God help all those who know not that they are created to be ALIVE."

**"God isn't the God of dead men, but the living. To him all are alive". (Luke 20:38 MSG)**

**THE LORD IS MY SHEPHERD I SHALL NOT WANT.**

**THE 23rd PSALM IS <u>MY STRENGTH!</u>**
**THE LORD IS MY STRENGTH!**
**THE LORD IS MY SHEPHERD!**

# 30 DAYS TO STRENGTH

## THE HEALING HAS BEGUN

**THIRTY DAYS TO STRENGTH** is designed to help you create healthy habits, to guide your spiritual journey to a life alive in God. Yes, you can with Gods' help lead yourselves out of ever valley. When you change your mind, you change your habits and you can change your life.

Begin the journey of spiritual healing where you are, open your mind and spirit receiving life as gift of God. Today, I believe in you and I am certain that you can achieve all that you set your mind and spirit to do. The strength of life must begin from within.

The good news is that if you can have one healthy (successful) day, then you simply repeat that day and it will turn into two, and two will turn to four. Before you know it, you will have completed one week and you are will be on your way to realizing the joy of a complete month of healthy living.

One healthy or successful month repeated can quickly three months and that can lead you into the year the changed your life. In these pages are the blue prints to actualize the dreams in your heart envisioned from the mind of God. You are stronger than you realize. Claim your strength, and witness the transformation that you and God together can manifest. Your new found strength (life) is only a day away, start today.

The longest journey begins with the first step; your challenge in faith today is to take that first step. When you pick up this book you took the first step, the healing has begun. The joy of life is not the arrival at the destination. The joy of life is the journey. As you travel, celebrate, pray some, play some, and always trust God in faith. God always knows what you need, the spirit will lead you, answer your questions and point the way to your life designed by God. Step out today, and travel the road in your strength.

Begin today, Claim your strength!

Write your vision of the life that you and God will create together.

_____

_____

_____

Write the daily habits you are going to practice to walk daily into you vision.

_____

_____

_____

# STRENGTH

## Day 1

## MY STRENGTH

**Today's Scripture**: "I have said this to you, so that you may have peace. In this world you face persecution. But take courage; I have conquered (overcome) the world!" (John 16:33)

**Today's Meditation:** Whenever there are competing concerns in your life, be sure to always put your relationship with God first. Seek God's direction in prayer knowing that you are a beloved child of God. Today, I begin the journey to claim my strength.

**Prayer** (Be still and listen for God)

_____

_____

**Personal Reflection**

   a. What do I hear God Saying?

   b. Where is God leading?

   c. What must I change or follow up today, to respond to God?

**Actions to take today:**

**Reflections of today's journey:**

**Today I Claim My Strength!**

## Day 2

### The Lord is one

**Today's Scripture:** "Jesus answered, "The first is, "hear, O Israel: the Lord our God, **the Lord is one**: you shall love the Lord your God with all your heart, and with all your soul, and with your entire mind, and with all your strength. The second is, "you shall love your neighbor as yourself.' There is no other commandment greater than these." (Mark 12:29-31)

**Today's Meditation:** "The Lord is one...Today, I am one with God. In the oneness of God is everything I need.

**Prayer** (Be still and listen for God)

_____

_____

**Personal Reflection**

    a. What do I hear God Saying?

    b. Where is God leading?

    c. What must I change or follow up today, to respond to God?

**Actions to take today:**

**Reflections of today's journey:**

**Today I Claim My Strength!**

## Day 3

## God's great gift

**Today's Scripture:** "Jesus answered, "The first is, "hear, O Israel: the Lord our God, the Lord is one: **you shall love the Lord your God with all your heart, and with all your soul, and with your entire mind, and with all your strength.** The second is, "you shall love your neighbor as yourself.' There is no other commandment greater than these." (Mark 12:29-31)

**Today's Meditation:** To know God is to love God. Love is not distant, love is up close, personal, Love calls for our attention, it invades our heart, our soul, our mind, our strength, and love is the greatest gift of all. Today, receive again, God's great gift.

**Prayer** (Be still and listen for God)

_____

_____

## Personal Reflection

a. What do I hear God Saying?

b. Where is God leading?

c. What must I change or follow up today, to respond to God?

**Actions to take today:**

**Reflections of today's journey:**

**Today I Claim My Strength!**

## Day 4

## My Neighbor

**Today's Scripture:** "Jesus answered, "The first is, "hear, O Israel: the Lord our God, the Lord is one: you shall love the Lord your God with all your heart, and with all your soul, and with your entire mind, and with all your strength. The second is, **"you shall love your neighbor as yourself**.' There is no other commandment greater than these." (Mark 12:29-31)

**Today's Meditation:** To love your neighbor is to recognize the divine spark that is within all of God's creation. To love your neighbor as yourself is to value, respect, and appreciate what God is doing in the ongoing act of creation. I mean you no harm, and I recognize that you are a child of God.

**Prayer** (Be still and listen for God)

_____

_____

**Personal Reflection**

    a. What do I hear God Saying?

    b. Where is God leading?

    c. What must I change or follow up today, to respond to God?

**Actions to take today:**

**Reflections of today's journey:**

**Today I Claim My Strength!**

## Day 5

## God Can

**Today's Scripture:** "Cast your burden on the Lord, and he will sustain you; ..." (Psalms 55:22)

**Today's Meditation:** Do not just cast your burden to the side, cast your burden on the Lord. Let the Lord help you in every challenge, God can bear every burden.

**Prayer** (Be still and listen for God)

_____

_____

## Personal Reflection

a. What do I hear God Saying?

b. Where is God leading?

c. What must I change or follow up today, to respond to God?

**Actions to take today:**

**Reflections of today's journey:**

**Today I Claim My Strength!**

## Day 6

## Strength

**Today's Scripture:** "He gives power to the faint, and strengthens the powerless." (Isaiah 40:29)

**Today's Meditation:** To know the strength of God, come to know the love of God.

**Prayer** (Be still and listen for God)

_____

_____

## Personal Reflection

a. What do I hear God Saying?

b. Where is God leading?

c. What must I change or follow up today, to respond to God?

**Actions to take today:**

**Reflections of today's journey:**

**Today I Claim My Strength!**

## Day 7

## A New Day

**Today's Scripture:** "...for the joy of the Lord is my strength." (Nehemiah 8:10)

**Today's Meditation:** Faith, hope, love, and joy are the watch words of daily living in Christ. Your strength is in the joy of the Lord. Rejoice in all that the Lord has provided, and saying thank you to what life brings today.

**Prayer** (Be still and listen for God)

_____

_____

## Personal Reflection

a. What do I hear God Saying?

b. Where is God leading?

c. What must I change or follow up today, to respond to God?

**Actions to take today:**

**Reflections of today's journey:**

**Today I Claim My Strength!**

## Day 8

## Receive the Promise

**Today's Scripture:** "For in him every one of God's promises is a "Yes." (2 Corinthians 1:20)

**Today's Meditation:** When the question is raised, is God able and willing to fulfill God's promise? The answer is yes and amen. Pray in the spirit, listening to God and receiving God's promise.

**Prayer** (Be still and listen for God)

_____

_____

**Personal Reflection**

a. What do I hear God Saying?

b. Where is God leading?

c. What must I change or follow up today, to respond to God?

**Actions to take today:**

**Reflections of today's journey:**

**Today I Claim My Strength!**

## Day 9

## Be Flexible

**Today's Scripture:** "Beloved, we are God's children; now what we will be has not yet been revealed. What we do know is this: when he is revealed, we will be life him, for we will see him as he is." (1 John 3:2)

**Today's Meditation:** Life in God is full of surprises. Live life not as an oak, strong, unbending; live as a reed, flexible, able to sway with the winds and storms of life. Even the mightiest of oaks will break when facing serve storms. Be flexible!

**Prayer** (Be still and listen for God)

_____

_____

## Personal Reflection

a. What do I hear God Saying?

b. Where is God leading?

c. What must I change or follow up today, to respond to God?

**Actions to take today:**

**Reflections of today's journey:**

**Today I Claim My Strength!**

## Day 10

### What's next?

**Today's Scripture:** "…Truly I tell you, unless you change and become like children, you will never enter the kingdom of heaven." (Matthew 18:3)

**Today's Meditation:** Life in God is spontaneous, joyful, and expectant, it is not that we are uncertain about God, we are just uncertain about what God is going to do next. What's next?

**Prayer** (Be still and listen for God)

_____

_____

**Personal Reflection**

a. What do I hear God Saying?

b. Where is God leading?

c. What must I change or follow up today, to respond to God?

**Actions to take today:**

**Reflections of today's journey:**

**Today I Claim My Strength!**

## Day 11

## Freedom

**Today's Scripture:** "For freedom Christ has set us free. Stand firm, therefore, and do not submit again to a yoke for slavery." (Galatians 5:1)

**Today's Meditation:** Patience is a virtual. Do not become anxious, when it appears your progress is moving ever so slow. The Kingdom is like the tiniest of seed sown, and will sprout, grow and produce to fruit of God in your life.

**Prayer** (Be still and listen for God)

_____

_____

## Personal Reflection

a. What do I hear God Saying?

b. Where is God leading?

c. What must I change or follow up today, to respond to God?

**Actions to take today:**

**Reflections of today's journey:**

**Today I Claim My Strength!**

## Day 12

## Trust

**Today's Scripture:** "Though he slay me yet will I trust him. (Job 13:15)

**Today's Meditation:** Trust can be so very difficult. Entrust your life to the hands of God. Maintain an intimate relationship with Jesus Christ. Perseverance of faith is to say, I will trust God.

**Prayer** (Be still and listen for God)

_____

_____

## Personal Reflection

a. What do I hear God Saying?

b. Where is God leading?

c. What must I change or follow up today, to respond to God?

**Actions to take today:**

**Reflections of today's journey:**

**Today I Claim My Strength!**

## Day 13

## My source

**Today's Scripture:** "…all my springs are in you." (Psalms 87:7)

**Today's Meditation:** Life, heath, and strength all flow from the abundant source of our creator. Today, we recognize the God is our source.

**Prayer** (Be still and listen for God)

_____

_____

## Personal Reflection

a. What do I hear God Saying?

b. Where is God leading?

c. What must I change or follow up today, to respond to God?

**Actions to take today**:

**Reflections of today's journey**:

**Today I Claim My Strength!**

## Day 14

## Mind

**Today's Scripture:** "Let this mind be in your which was also in Christ Jesus." (Philippians 2:5)

**Today's Meditation:** The Christian life is one of spiritual courage and determination. It is hungering and thirsting after the very mind of Christ.

**Prayer** (Be still and listen for God)

_____

_____

## Personal Reflection

a. What do I hear God Saying?

b. Where is God leading?

c. What must I change or follow up today, to respond to God?

**Actions to take today:**

**Reflections of today's journey:**

**Today I Claim My Strength!**

## Day 15

## Compelled

**Today's Scripture:** "The Love of Christ compels us…." (2 Corinthians 5:14)

**Today's Meditation:** Love is the most powerful force in the universe. We are taught in scripture that "God is Love". All of my relationships must be lived out in the reality that I am in a loving relationship with God. Today, I will love God, love others, and follow Jesus.

**Prayer** (Be still and listen for God)

_____

_____

## Personal Reflection

a. What do I hear God Saying?

b. Where is God leading?

c. What must I change or follow up today, to respond to God?

**Actions to take today:**

**Reflections of today's journey:**

**Today I Claim My Strength!**

# Day 16

## Prayer

**Today's Scripture:** Pray without ceasing." (1 Thessalonians 5:17)

**Today's Meditation:** Think of prayer as the breath in the lungs and the blood for the heart. Our blood flows and our breathing continues "without ceasing"; we are not even conscious of it, but it never stops. Prayer is the life of the believer.

---

**Prayer** (Be still and listen for God)

_____

_____

## Personal Reflection

a. What do I hear God Saying?

b. Where is God leading?

c. What must I change or follow up today, to respond to God?

**Actions to take today:**

**Reflections of today's journey:**

**Today I Claim My Strength!**

# Day 17

## Seek

**Today's Scripture:** "For every one that asks receives, and everyone who searches finds, and for everyone who knocks, the door will be opened." (Matthew 7:8)

**Today's Meditation:** Yes, God does answer prayer, not always is the evidence of that answered prayer easily discernible. The promise of God is seek and you will find, knock and the door will be opened. Do not give up. Keep seeing, keep knocking and the door will be opened.

---

**Prayer** (Be still and listen for God)

_____

_____

**Personal Reflection**

a. What do I hear God Saying?

b. Where is God leading?

c. What must I change or follow up today, to respond to God?

---

**Actions to take today:**

**Reflections of today's journey:**

**Today I Claim My Strength!**

## Day 18

## My Help

**Today's Scripture:** "The Lord is my helper: the Lord is with them that uphold my soul." (Psalms 54:4)

**Today's Meditation:** I will not live in fear. I will not become obsessed with apprehension. I will remember God's Word of presence. I will listen for the guiding voice of God. I will live with Godly courage. I am not alone.

---

**Prayer** (Be still and listen for God)

_____

_____

## Personal Reflection

a. What do I hear God Saying?

b. Where is God leading?

c. What must I change or follow up today, to respond to God?

---

**Actions to take today:**

**Reflections of today's journey:**

**Today I Claim My Strength!**

# Day 19

## Abide

**Today's Scripture:** "Abide in me as I abide in you, just as the branch cannot bear fruit by itself unless it abides in the vine, neither can you unless you abide in me." (John 15:4)

**Today's Meditation:** It is not my work, my service, my sacrifice or even my work for the Lord, none of these that should exert the ultimate power over my life. It is my relationship with Christ. Am I abiding in the Lord daily!

**Prayer** (Be still and listen for God)

_____

_____

**Personal Reflection**

a. What do I hear God Saying?

b. Where is God leading?

c. What must I change or follow up today, to respond to

God?

**Actions to take today:**

**Reflections of today's journey:**

**Today I Claim My Strength!**

## Day 20

## Walk with God

**Today's Scripture:** "Which one of you, intending to build a tower, does not sit down first and court the cost, whether he has enough to finish..." (Luke 14:28)

**Today's Meditation:** Ours is the challenge to finish strong. God who began a good work in you will see it to completion. Walk in the vision of God for your life. Today, I will finish strong.

**Prayer** (Be still and listen for God)

_____

_____

## Personal Reflection

a. What do I hear God Saying?

b. Where is God leading?

c. What must I change or follow up today, to respond to God?

**Actions to take today:**

**Reflections of today's journey:**

**Today I Claim My Strength!**

## Day 21

## Follow Me

**Today's Scripture:** "...come follow me." (Luke 18:22)

**Today's Meditation:** The invitation of Jesus to come to him is extend again and again. It is Jesus' call to experience the Kingdom of God while we are yet in the land of the living. Accept Jesus' invitation and never turn back. Today, I will follow Jesus. Loving God, loving others and following Jesus.

**Prayer** (Be still and listen for God)

_____

_____

## Personal Reflection

a. What do I hear God Saying?

b. Where is God leading?

c. What must I change or follow up today, to respond to God?

186

**Actions to take today:**

**Reflections of today's journey:**

**Today I Claim My Strength!**

## Day 22

## The Towel of Humanly

**Today's Scripture:** "Jesus, knowing that the Father had given all things into his hands, and that he had come from God and was going to God, got up from the table, took off his outer rob, and tied a towel around himself.  Then he poured water into a basin and began to wash the disciples' feet and to wipe them with the towel that was tied around him." (John 13:3-5)

**Today's Meditation:**  Service to God every day is my intention, in the small act of kindness; a kind embrace, a smile, becoming the loving presence of God.  Jesus molded for his disciples that those who would lead must humble themselves and become servant. I am a servant to all humanity.

**Prayer** (Be still and listen for God)

_____

_____

**Personal Reflection**

a. What do I hear God Saying?

b. Where is God leading?

c. What must I change or follow up today, to respond to

God?

**Actions to take today**:

**Reflections of today's journey**:

**Today I Claim My Strength!**

## Day 23

## Light

**Today's Scripture:** "...you are called out of the darkness into his marvelous light." (1 Peter 2:9)

**Today's Meditation:** The light of God shines in the mist of darkness. In the beginning God said let there be light. We are told that Jesus is the light of the world. The light shined in the darkness and the darkness did not overcome it.

**Prayer** (Be still and listen for God)

_____

_____

**Personal Reflection**

a. What do I hear God Saying?

b. Where is God leading?

c. What must I change or follow up today, to respond to God?

**Actions to take today:**

**Reflections of today's journey:**

**Today I Claim My Strength!**

# Day 24

## Living Water

**Today's Scripture:** "...Out of the believer's heart shall flow rivers of living water." (John 7:38)

**Today's Meditation:** Regardless of your circumstance, or whoever you encounter today remember Christ is your source. It is through our right relationship with Christ that rivers of living water will flow out of our hearts.

**Prayer** (Be still and listen for God)

_____

_____

**Personal Reflection**

a. What do I hear God Saying?

b. Where is God leading?

c. What must I change or follow up today, to respond to God?

**Actions to take today:**

**Reflections of today's journey:**

**Today I Claim My Strength!**

# Day 25

## Spirit and Life

**Today's Scripture:** ".., The words that I have spoken to you are spirit and life." (John 6:63)

**Today's Meditation:** The word of God is living word. The word became flesh and lived among us, and we have seen his glory, the glory as of a father's only son, full of grace and truth. It is through Gods Word and the presence of the spirit we have life. The Spirit is life and life is the Spirit.

**Prayer** (Be still and listen for God)

_____

_____

## Personal Reflection

a. What do I hear God Saying?

b. Where is God leading?

c. What must I change or follow up today, to respond to God?

**Actions to take today:**

**Reflections of today's journey:**

**Today I Claim My Strength!**

## Day 26

## Bethel

**Today's Scripture:** "From there he moved on to the hill country on the east of Bethel, and pitched his tent, with Bethel on the west and Ai on the east; and there he built an altar to the Lord and invoked the name of the Lord." (Genesis 12:8)

**Today's Meditation:** Bethel is the symbol of fellowship with God. Ai is the symbol of the world. Between these two extremes, Abram pitched his tent; it is between these two extremes that we live out our lives. We live with the challenges of this world but straining toward a city not made by human hands.

**Prayer** (Be still and listen for God)

_____

_____

## Personal Reflection

a. What do I hear God Saying?

b. Where is God leading?

c. What must I change or follow up today, to respond to God?

**Actions to take today:**

**Reflections of today's journey:**

**Today I Claim My Strength!**

## Day 27

## My Advocate

**Today's Scripture:** "But the Advocate, the Holy Spirit, whom the Father will send in my name, will teach you everything, and remind you of all that I have said to you." (John 14:26)

**Today's Meditation:** "Temptation, disappointment, broken relationship, constantly questioned, only after the coming of the Holy Spirit did the disciples begin to understand the purpose of God. The Holy Spirit is your advocate.

**Prayer** (Be still and listen for God)

_____

_____

**Personal Reflection**

a. What do I hear God Saying?

b. Where is God leading?

c. What must I change or follow up today, to respond to God?

**Actions to take today:**

**Reflections of today's journey:**

**Today I Claim My Strength!**

## Day 28

## Press On

**Today's Scripture:** *"Not that I have already obtained this or have already reached my goal, but I press on to make it my own, because Christ Jesus has made me his own"* *(Philippians 3:12).*

**Today's Meditation:** Your life today is in the very hands of God. Purpose in your heart that as God holds on to you, you will hold on to God. Press through ever obstacle you have, you are stronger than you think. Today, claim your strength.

**Prayer** (Be still and listen for God)

_____

_____

**Personal Reflection**

a. What do I hear God Saying?

b. Where is God leading?

c. What must I change or follow up today, to respond to God?

**Actions to take today**:

**Reflections of today's journey**:

**Today I Claim My Strength!**

# Day 29

## Dream Again

**Today's Scripture:** *"We know that all things work together for good to those who love God, who are called according to his purpose" (Romans 8:28).*

**Today's Meditation:** Be faithful, not just to your health, relationships, work and others, be faithful to God. Today, be faithful to the dream of God that has been birthed in you. I will dream again.

**Prayer** (Be still and listen for God)

_____

_____

## Personal Reflection

a. What do I hear God Saying?

b. Where is God leading?

c. What must I change or follow up today, to respond to God?

**Actions to take today**:

**Reflections of today's journey**:

**Today I Claim My Strength!**

## Day 30

## My Joy

**Today's Scripture**: "*These things I have spoken to you, that My joy may remain in you, and that your joy may be full*" *(John 15:11).*

**Today's Meditation**: Joy, joy, joy: pure, simple, unencumbered joy is what Jesus brings to those who choose to walk with him. This joy I have the world did not give it to me and the world cannot take it way. Live in joy, you have made it – celebrate.

**Prayer** (Be still and listen for God)

_____

_____

**Personal Reflection**

a. What do I hear God Saying?

b. Where is God leading?

c. What must I change or follow up today, to respond to God?

**Actions to take today**:

**Reflections of today's journey**:

**Today I Claim My Strength!**

# ABOUT THE AUTHOR

**Dr. Casey R. Kimbrough** serves as the Senior Pastor of The Mount Carmel Baptist Church Charlotte, North Carolina and Adjunct professor at Johnson C. Smith University.  He got his start while serving as a student Chaplin at The University of Rochester while attending Colgate Rochester Crozer Divinity School in Rochester, New York.  He has also served in many community leadership positions and continues to mentor young leaders.  Most recently, he has added author to list of accomplishments, with the publication of his new book "Strength".  He spends most of his time as a servant leader, pouring into the lives of others.  His unique ability to bring together the analytical skills of an engineer and the sensitivity of a spiritual leader set him apart.  Recognized as an innovator in productivity, servant leadership and spiritual direction his voice is in great demand.  He speaks on these topics to churches, communities and corporations, at various conferences.
He and his wife, LeeDonna make their home on Charlotte, North Carolina.

Contact Information:
Rev. Dr. Casey R. Kimbrough
caseykimbrough@gmail.com
Aliveteachingministries.com
DrK@aliveteachingministries.com

Mount Carmel Baptist Church
7237 Tuckaseegee Road
Charlotte, North Carolina 28269
Mountcarmelbaptistchurch-nc.org
Pastork@mountcarmelbaptist-nc.org

# STRENGTH